T0128529

A SHATTERED
CHILD

A SHATTERED
CHILD

Bruised but not Broken

TAMMY HICKSON

authorHOUSE®

AuthorHouse™
1663 Liberty Drive
Bloomington, IN 47403
www.authorhouse.com
Phone: 1-800-839-8640

First published by AuthorHouse   04/14/2012

ISBN: 978-1-4685-8880-4 (sc)
ISBN: 978-1-4685-8881-1 (e)

Library of Congress Control Number: 2012906903

CONTENTS

This book is dedicated to my four wonderful children: De'Marcus, Casey, Danielle, and KeAlbre'tt. Who are the soul winners of my heart. They believed in me as I went through my journey in life and stood beside me every step of the way. I'm grateful for each and every one of you, with the faith each of you had in me made me fight to be who I am today. I love you endlessy, and Thank You!

Also I wrote this book in MEMORY of my Mother, (the late) Pamela J. Casey-Gilmore. Who birthed me, raised me, and gave me direction in areas of life and taught me how to be strong, to believe and trust in God. I will be forever grateful for her wisdom that she shared with me.

Rest in Heaven my beautiful Angel . . .

As I began to write this book, all the intentions that I had has been rearranged. I have rewritten this book three times and it's because what I tried to make the book be, isn't what it was suppose to be. So as you read and go on this Journey with me, I pray that it reaches your heart, and that it heals someone that has gone and is going through the same things that I have gone through, and know that there is a God, and that he does live, and that he is the source of your healing. Rather the scars are fresh, or they have been deeply embedded in you. God is a healer and he will take all the pain away if you allow him to.

Born October 15th, 1970 to the late Pamela Casey-Gilmore and the late Dwight Davis. It was then that I would begin my life. A healthy baby girl that was loved by everyone. Family and close friends of the family. They say I never met a stranger. Life was good as we shared housing with my grandmother because my Mama was just a young girl herself. At the age of 14 years old, she would give birth to me. And my grandmother would help raise me. I remember our home being the place where everyone would come together and have a good time. There would be loud music, food being cooked, finger popping, singing and dancing, just family and friends being together enjoying one another. It seems that we had the best spot in our little town. My family may not have had millions of dollars, and houses on the hill with white pickett fences, but we had LOVE and it was displayed for everyone to see and feel. Growing up in that environment made me love more and want to be loved more. That type of love resides in my heart today, even though mine has been stolen or abused more than a few times, I still find the courage to give it. In the midst of me growing up, I had a lot of friends. A lot that I went to school with, and family the same age as me. One particular cousin I have and growing up with, we spent a lot of time together. We would spend countless hours on the back porch eating salad dressing and crackers. It was our favorite. The playground would be full of us running around having fun, chasing after one another, and simply being the kids we were. But even before that, when I was the age of two there would be a terrible car accident that would cause me to be severely injured. As I went through the windshield of the car, my forehead would be busted open, and my right ear would be split completely in half to the point it had to be sewed back together. By the grace of God, I would live and be ok. I believe that's the day I became a fighter. A fighter for life, a fighter for what was mine, a fighter for what I deserved in life. Even though at times I didn't have a lot of strength to fight, somewhere somehow I would mustard enough up to keep on going. Life has taught me a lot of things, kind and unkind. The good and the ugly, most definitely the bitter with the sweet. It has showed me so much, that I've had to learn how to duck and dodge things that came my way, in a bad way. Especially the things that came into my life to harm me on purpose. Never understanding how people could come with intent to harm, blew my mind every time it happened. By me being a kind hearted person and always eagered to help, I couldn't imagine someone else being mischieveous and under handing to knock other people down to make themselves appear to be the better person. It didn't feel good to me to be done that way, and God bless the hearts of the people that betrayed me.

"A SHATTERED CHILD"

(bruised but not Broken)

As a young child, I could remember everyone telling me how I was a big chunky healthy baby, that use to sit in the middle of the dinner table and eat anything that I wanted to eat, because everybody had me spoiled like that. I remember growing up in an apartment with my Grandmother, my mama, and my uncles. And later it would be my baby sister. As my memory takes me back, I can visualize my mama's bedroom. It had such a sweet smell. We slept in a full size canopy bed, with lavender bedding that made it all prettied up. What I remember the most is the cedar chest that would sit at the foot of the bed on the floor. It's as if I can still smell the cedar when the top was opened. It always made me feel safe. From what I've been told by a lot of people, everybody loved me and they would love on me, give me kisses all the time and pinch on my fat jaws, and all the while feeding me. My childhood was good and it was because I sheltered a lot of things out of it while I was growing up. A lot of things that I had been through, no one knew because I never told. My childhood friends were wonderful, and we all use to get out on the playground and play until the sun was going down. We would love to play kickball, hide and go seek, tag, and other fun games that were out back then. Attending the schools together, we literally did everything together. A lot of time was spent between one cousin and I. we would sit on the back stoop and eat salad dressing(sandwich spread)and crackers. We would eat corn starch right out the box, the crazy things we would eat. This particular cousin and I would spend time together even when me and my other family and friends wouldn't. I would even go with her to her babysitters house, just so she would have someone to play with while she was there. From all those childhood memories from then to now we still reminisce on the younger years of our lives time to time.

During those times my Granny would always have something going on at our home. It was always some type of gathering of friends and family, cooking, music, and drinking. It's as if our house was the love house for everyone to join in and have a good time. Some might say that at that time I was too young to know what was going on. Especially to know it in such details. Please understand that God has taken me back to the age of three years old to write this book. So as you read, know that I was lead by God to have this wonderful experience to share my life's story with you. When I tell you that people were at our house all the time day in, and day out. Finger popping, lipstick wearing, fried chicken eating, laughing, and a whole lot of good times. I learned later in life that it's what our family was known for, having a good time no matter what. They didn't have mansions on a hill, or millions of dollars in their pockets, but my family was truly that FAMILY. And it was constantly a closeness.

As the good times were rolling on, some things were beginning to transpire that had no business happening. Laying in bed to sleep at night while the party was going on downstairs under me, I would begin to be violated in a way that I could never understand why it was being done to me. How could anyone in their sane mind do the things that were done to me at the young age that I was. He was a wolf that dressed himself in sheep's clothing to the family, so that they would view him in a respectful way. But all the while he was coming up stairs pretending to use the bathroom, but take advantage of me. Thinking back on those incidents, I can't understand how no one else never came to use the bathroom during that time to catch him doing what he was doing. Wasn't anyone else tipsy enough to have to pee back to back? Didn't anyone ever notice that this particular person would be gone for too long from amongst everyone else? Did I never get checked on while I was sleeping to make sure I was alright? My mind still ask the questions of how this was allowed to happen right under everyone else noses. It was too many people in the house for someone not to see what was going on. Why was this man doing evil things to me, that I had no idea about anyway? Understanding to his actions wasn't a part for me to play, because I was a baby myself. And as I lay there my innocence was being stripped from me night after night after night. Was the music so loud that no one heard my silent screams that were being thrust from my mouth? My God where was my help? But never the less time proceeded to carry on. It was time for me enter into pre-school and continue to be around all my friends. In the classroom playing dress-up and pretending we were cooking meals for our families. Doing art project and other things that the teacher would assign for us. I loved it because it took my focus off all the bad things in life. It was a way for me to release without even knowing that's what I was doing. It was such good times, joyful times, innocent times. Back then everyone looked out for each other. That's how close most of us were. Believe it or not, I was the quite one of us all (I know you can't tell it today) I giggled to myself as I wrote this, because to know me today; I am forth coming, strong minded, and very, very, outspoken. In saying that, I wonder if all I went through made me that way?

As more time went on, I merged into grade school. The first day that I was taken to school by my mama, we walked in and the teacher is standing there greeting all the parents and the other students that came through the door. Now mind you that I was so spoiled that for me to venture off into a new surrounding didn't set well with me. I didn't want to stay, but I know I had to. As my mama turned to walk out the class, I started to cry and didn't want her to leave me there with those people. And though most of them were my friends already, I just wasn't ready for the change. So I immediately ran out of the classroom and out the building, down the sidewalk and across the street, next thing I know I'm running all the way back home with tears in my eyes wanting my mama and granny. That was an upsetting day for me, but I can't remember if I was able to stay home or made to go back to school. After a few days of going and getting use to everything, I started to settle in with my new class and other students and connecting back with my old friends and family. Soon it would be where all the good times took place. And my teacher was the best teacher ever. She was/is the sweetest lady I know. She treated us good and made sure that we were getting our lessons along with staying out of trouble. A God fearing woman she has always been, and has stood through a lot of trials and tribulations. At the end of it all, she is still standing. One day while entering the classroom I went into the coat closet to hang my coat. A minute later my cousin came into the closet also, and was talking with me as if everything was fine. I can't remember if we had an argument (which I don't think we did) she was just devious like that. But anyway, she came towards me with a pencil and proceeded to stab me in the back with it. I didn't know what was going on or why she would even do a thing such as that. As I started to scream out, the teacher came running in the closet to see what was happening. She seen my cousin as she began to back away from me, and I told her what had just happened and she sent her to the principal's office. Good thing I wasn't seriously hurt, even though it did leave a puncture mark.

I loved school back then, and lunch was a fun time; and delicious all at the same time. Our lunch lady was so nice to us. In fact; I've never had a lunch lady like her ever again. She was so sweet and treated us as if we belonged to her. Always wore a smile on her face and always happy. At least that's how she would seem. A very small petite woman and she wore her hair big and teased. It was white with silver tint to it, and she kept a net on it at all times. Lord knows I remember everything about her. Her kindness went along way in that school, seems hers made up for the ones that weren't so nice. After lunch we would have recess. Talking about the best part of the day besides lunch (giggles), oh boy me and my friends couldn't wait for that to come around. We would play hard and have so much fun, to the point of when it was time to go back to class, we didn't want to. But knowing that we had to; we would slowly drag our feet to head back to the classroom. It was fun living my life as a kid, but only certain times though. Because of things that I was going through at such an early age. I also was going through a phase where I wanted to be like other little girls around me. Not knowing what I was asking for, without asking. Progressing on into higher grades, that by third grade a lot of the girls were already going into puberty. A few had developed breast and big butts, so I started to wonder what it would be like to have those things too. Coming to school seeing that on a day to day basis, made my mind assume more. So I started to stuff my shirts with toilet paper, to make it seem that I was developing too. Trying to fit in with everyone else, when I should have left well enough alone. Being a child is the most important years of a child's life, but when it has been secretly betrayed what do you do with it? When you don't have anyone to instill those things in you, so that you can learn from it, it makes it hard not to know not to follow anyone else, and just be yourself. It went on for a long period of time, before I stopped stuffing. Our third grade teacher was hard on us, and I honestly don't think it was to make us better individuals, it was that she was simply a mean old lady. I had never seen a face that was so wrinkled and drown up. It seemed she was out to get us with every move that we made. Almost as she would sit back and wait for us to mess up, and we would do just that . . . MESS UP! She would sit back, twiddle her fingers, and wait so she could paddle us, and then with her famous wooden ruler, she would strike us on the inside of our hands with that. It would sting like crazy. And I guess she wasn't trying to spare the rod and spoil the child, (giggles).

We must know that God is the opposite, he doesn't sit back and wait for us to mess up. He's there to let us know that we DON'T have to mess up, but when we do he is there and will help us not knock us down. He will help us to turn from our ungodly ways, if we want him to. Eventually I had to changes schools, and started with another different group of people. They as well were family and friends, so I fit right in with them too. Definitely went through some crazy times there also. Still hadn't found my own identity, it caused me to continue to run in behind people trying to be like them. WRONG MOVE! I started to get into it with my teachers and other students in general. I kept punishment going on for myself because I was always into something. One teacher in particular had a punishment for us that was called the duck walk. It was were we had to squat down in position and walk like a duck. When I tell you that it was painful, words can not explain. Going through life with no sense of direction and no clue of knowing how to be responsible, I was making poor decisions for my life. My intentions of writing in this format of going forward, then backing up a bit is to give you a feel of every part of my life, as much as I can. It's to gear you up for the deeper intense stories to come. Just stay with me and I will take you exactly where you need to be at the moment you need to be there. With graduating fifth grade and enter into middle school, was somewhat intimidating for me. I was not ready to go into anything more challenging for my brain. I know it meant more homework, harder tasks to follow, and more complications. (and that is exactly how we do with the assignments from God). We are fine as long as what he gives us don't take us out of our comfort zone. As soon as he begin to pull us out of the box, we start to feel intimidation coming on, because we are fearful of the unknown. We at times don't realize that if he's taking us out of certain situations, then he's going to be there for us. God is always there to guide and lead us, he will never leave nor forsake us. Just as the teachers were going to be there to help me in middle school. I had to learn to trust them, simply the goodness of God. No doubt that the sixth through eighth grade was a struggle for me. Eventually school became just a place for me to go hang out with my friends, doing little to no lessons at all. While I was busy being a class clown and showing off for all the other students, they were moving right along with doing their homework and listening to the teachers. To where I would have to cram at the last minute to be able to get passing grades. I would sit in class not paying attention to what the teacher was talking about, and I would write letters so I could pass them out during class changes in the hall. Again I didn't have anyone to guide me or teach me. I lived in the principal's office more than in the classroom. During that time my behavior wasn't connected to what was going on with me behind closed doors. My smile and my people person ways never let anyone know that, things were happening to me. Becoming a follower rather than a leader, I was able to do just what I wanted to do. When I figured out that no one was paying attention to me because they were doing their own thing, that's when I did my own thing too. I wanted to fit in, and I wanted others to like me, so whatever it took to be a part of the team, I did it. I acted out in hurt and was seeking that attention and affection that I was lacking at home. I didn't like anyone being mad at me, so pleasing people would be at the top of my list.

I carried a huge chip on my shoulder for most part of my life. Some of it came from my dad not being there for me, like he could have been. Other reasons were the lack of affection of my mother. I knew she loved me, but she wasn't a person that showed her emotions. My sisters and brother knew she loved us because of the way she took care of us, but she never said it too often. She made sure we had what we needed and most of what we wanted. But to embrace us and tell us "I love you", no that rarely happened. As I said about my dad, I feel he could have put in more time with me. My granny says that he did, but as I told her it must have been when I wasn't old enough to remember, because what I do remember . . . he wasn't there. When I got old enough to see things for myself and come to my own conclusions, it was then that I realized that he thought being around me would involve him giving me money, so I guess that's why he stayed away the way that he did. If my mouth looked as if it was going to speak the word money, he would quickly say "well baby girl, I ain't got no money bills were due". I would shake my head and think (this grown man is really missing the respecting point of the father/daughter relationship). I felt like things between us could have been much better if only he had took the time to do so. It behooved me how we lived in the same city, same state, and barely saw one another, unless I took the lead to make it happen. Even when I did go to him, it was short visits because he always had something more important to do. My feelings and emotions are mixed up about him still. And he has passed on and everything. I now know that growing up and being rebellious and out being with different men, was from the lack of my father being in my life. It would be times that I wanted to hear my dad say he loved me, he never would unless I told him first. It's the very reason I say to men young and old, it is very important that you be good father's to your children, because it can leave a huge scare on that child's heart. And it will make the child act in ways that would normally not be displayed, had dad been there. Most people think that the boys are the most important to be raised with a father . . . . I'm here to tell you that, it's just as important for girls too. Wether male or female, a father should teach them good things, lead them in the right direction, and teach them to be a responsible mom or dad themselves one day. The more I learn each day and grow closer to God, I begin to understand that in order to know and learn you have to have someone to get something from. Even when our parents don't know, it's because they themselves didn't have anyone to learn from either. So there comes a time when we have to ask, DO WE BLAME OUR PARENTS? It's really a tricky question, because we say it starts at home with teaching children the ways of life. Would that be some sort of contradiction? So with that being said, we as parents need to teach our children carefully with education and with the wars of life. Let them know that everything is not going to be peaches and cream along the journey, but teach them that they have to trust God enough to get through it. A person is NEVER too old to learn, and I don't consider a question to be dumb if you don't know. We don't know everything, and it's the very reason God allows different people to go through different things, so we may learn from one another. Moving right along. My mother was the sweetest person in my book. She would give someone the shirt off of her back if she had to. It would be times that people would wrong her, and she would turn right around and give them a helping hand. I never understood her motive of doing such of a thing, of blessing her enemies. Until, I had gotten a little older. She would tell me to treat people well, no matter if they did the same to me in return. She really led that statement by example, which was hard for me to do. Because if I helped someone and went out of my way only to have someone act any other way than grateful, it became a problem. During my childhood days my mom wasn't saved with the Lord, but she displayed the type of love he had to other people. And that was no matter the circumstances, LOVE anyway. Before I didn't understand the meaning of (turn the other cheek), because I would be ready to slap a cheek, especially when someone messed with my mom in the wrong way. A lot of times I would question God and ask him, why did he make my heart as good as he did? Even though I would be angry at folk, I would still treat them good and I didn't like being good to someone that wasn't good to me. It's so many things in life that God allows to happen to us, that we will probably never understand. But we have to know that it's all for some type of reason. So no matter what we go through or IS going through, readers you have to know that there IS a GOD, and he can bring you through anything if you would just trust him. He will provide deliverance on your behalf also. I am a witness to what he can do, because he has brought me from a mighty long way, and I am still aiming everyday to be the best that I can be, concerning

God. As I had spoken before, my mom wasn't the best at showing her emotions but I did learn a lot from her.

"WHEN YOU THINK YOU HAVE IT ALL IN THE BAG, AND THE BAG RIPS WITHOUT YOU KNOWING IT, UNTIL YOU'RE TOO FAR ALONG TO TURN AROUND AND PICK IT ALL UP AGAIN". I said that to say, even though we go through life and learn things, it's at our best interest to keep that information aboard our brain. Because loosing vital partaking of what we have, it somewhat damages what we have taken the time to absorb. Then we linger on what has been given, before we know it, we've lost it. Temptations are all about the earth, and it will get the best of you if you don't know how to handle it. I assume that's the reason cold-hearted behavior was done to me, OR was it that at all? Can you tell me what is so tempting of a three year old child, to a grown over aged man? At that age she is most definitely innocent. A baby that hasn't formed into feminine maturity yet, so I ask again . . . WHAT IS SO TEMPTING? I've lived many of my years with the perception that everyone wanted Tammy. It caused to believe that I was invincible, couldn't be touched. Don't get me wrong, I am a beautiful person but I had to know that my beauty stemmed from the inside out, and I didn't know that at the time. I would have more than my share at a time of men. I always kept a spare (because I thought that's what I had to do). And it was in case one or another didn't want to act right. I remembering having a guy for each day of the week, not meaning that I had seven different men but I would have about three on standby. It would be the lifestyle for me to live for a long time, and it didn't phase me, because I thought I was doing big things. What was I to know? I wasn't taught not to record my life in such a manner of what I was doing. I would do as I was pleased, with no boundaries. I lived as if nothing matter, and truth be told it didn't. I stayed numb for most part of living, nothing took effect on way or another. If I felt like something or someone was going to hurt me, it didn't matter because I had already positioned myself for the fall anyway. Failure always played a part in whatever I did, because I didn't know how to fight and make things right for me. I was what everybody said I was, even if it meant me being a failure, SO BE IT! For the ones that are reading my book, let me take a moment to encourage you.

1. ALWAYS CHOOSE GOD.
2. BE YOUR OWN VOICE IN WHAT'S BEST FOR YOU.
3. REALIZE THAT ONLY "YOU" CAN STOP YOU.
4. LAST BUT NOT LEAST, LOVE YOURSELF NO MATTER WHAT.

Mama was a strong woman in different aspects of her life. She was strong in the survival sense. She had a lot of street knowledge, and she knew how to get out there and make a way for whatever a way needed to be made for. It didn't matter, she never let us be without. And if we were without, trust me we didn't know it. It's amazing how I never really seen her crack under pressure. I can't remember a time hearing her say "I don't know how we're going to make it". In my eyes my mama was superwoman, and that made her my SHERO. It didn't too much matter that she didn't teach me much about life, her being my mother was enough for me at that time. She never left us, she never turned her back on us, she showed us what staying in the fight was all about. Never let us see her sweat. Such a strong woman, and she was our woman. I distinctly remember an argument that I had with a woman about numerous of things, but one thing that stood out to me the most, is when she said "YO MAMMIE ON DRUGS"! And I didn't let that statement get to me, because my perception of being on drugs is that, you pawn valuable belongings, and you neglect the important things in life, and you don't worry about the well being of your children. Well that was not the case at all with my mama, she did the opposite. She held it down for us, we didn't see her slip off her feet. I said the woman, if my mama is on drugs we don't know it and we are not suffering from it. I didn't know how to feel about it after that. Because now I'm wondering if what the lady said was true. No matter what my mom did, I always defended her. She was an outgoing person and she was a people person, so when she got pregnant with my little brother it sadden me, because deep down inside, I knew I would have to be the one to take care of him. So for a new addition to be added to our family was a bitter/sweet feeling. Because, mama stayed gone a lot. We would carry on with life as normal while she was carrying him inside her. I loved her so much, because watching her it taught me how to be protective. But when she got mad, she was mad. But all in all she was gentle as a dove. I notice the older I get, that more like her in a lot of my ways. She was a little rough around the edges in the tone of her voice. I find myself being the very same way, having the authorative tone in my voice, people tend to take u the wrong way. But once they really get to know you, they see that it's not your personality at all. My mom lived her life and didn't care what nobody else said or thought about it. I now realize that she probably was living out of hurt of her life and bad things that had happened to her. Growing up without her dad, raised in a single parent home and getting pregnant, and having me at the age of fourteen, I'm sure it's were mental behavior came from for her. Raising four children wasn't easy for her, but she made everything good for us though.

I want to explain something that most people don't understand. Even during the times that we share a relationship with a partner, it doesn't mean that we are not alone. We as people will go through life and live it as if everything is alright, or that we are fulfilled because we have a certain somebody to share companionship with. When the truth is . . . we are so lonely and broken on the inside. It's the way I have lived my live for 37 years. Because from age three, I have had to cover my life in order to cope with it as far as I could. To make me feel as if I was fine. It became so routine that it was a part of my being, and it was normal to me. But because of the grace of God, he saw me through every day. He didn't leave me, nor let death take life from me. Always wondering why God protected me, when I felt I wasn't worth saving from all I had been through. Then, again who am I to question him about what he does for anybody, including me?

When I speak on my terrible life, I tell you that it has taught me to value it more, because I eventually realized that I was worth living to make things better for myself. Again as I always say, life kept moving. I started to attend church on a regular basis. Started hearing the word of God and understanding it. I've had many to speak over my life and tell the promises that he has in store for me, I wanted to live that "free" life so bad. I knew I had a lot more demons to battle within myself, but God would be the one to help me make a change from that hindering spirit. My pastor at that time was preaching a sermon, one Sunday morning. And it was a bout walking in your destiny. He said that we are PURPOSELY CREATED-CREATED FOR A PURPOSE. And when I heard those words, I knew I had a chance. That word hit me like whoa! And from that day forward I took that and kept that word in my heart. My heart's desire is to live for the will of God concerning my well being. God had given me a scripture that was fitting for my life. Actually he gave me two, because he used my daughter one time to give me a scripture. And it was (ACTS 3:1-10). Where it speaks of the lame man lying at the gate of beautiful begging as people were coming and going. But when I first read that, I didn't see how it was transparent to my life. But the word crippled is what God wanted me to focus on, because it was as if I had been living crippled for a long time, and didn't have to be living that way at all. Can any of you relate to that? Then God gave me (JEREMIAH 29:14. I will be found by you declares the Lord, and will bring you back from captivity. I will gather you from all the nations and places where I banished you, declares the Lord. And will bring you back from the place from which I carried you into exile). Those words were as sweet as honey from a honey comb. I try to always refer back to that when doubt starts to come upon me. Because life gets hard to keep going sometimes, and we all need a little reminder on what's really important. Let me turn the story back to when I was age thirteen years old, and that's when I had my first consensual sexual experience. As I would think to myself, thirteen certainly can't be right to be having these type of relationships because I was still very young aged. It was then that I started to get into relationships with different boys my age, and some even a little older as well. We all were already friends and we ran around in the same circles and it was easier to hook up that way. I was never taught NOT to have sex. Even though I would hear people talk about it, but no one ever took time to sat down and go through that with me. So it was something that I wanted to go out and experiment with. I had already been tampered with anyway, so how much more harm could it do? The guy and me ended up in a little crushed filled relationship, and even after the break up we remained friends. But I kept dating other guys or "boys", if you will. I wonder why we as a people are that way with God? We are down to ride with him in a long relationship as long as things are going good, but as soon as something is misunderstood

(from our thinking) then we want to jump ship. And we will find something or someone else to pacify our time. Life is a learning experience and we are suppose to be learning and growing as we go. A lot of times we don't get it. We "MUST" come to realization that God is our EVERYTHING, and no matter what, he will always be there for us. Sometimes it takes a while to figure life out, and we hinder what God has set up for us. But when we finally grab hold to that thing, it becomes more powerful than we could ever imagine. Being sexual active before time, will certainly block blessings that God has for you/us. It is then, that we have to start doing things in a different way to get the gifts that are ours, and only God has them for us. When we think differently, we can perceive things differently.

I had a best friend in my life back then, and either one of us knew that God had such a strong calling on our lives. We lived foot loose and fancy free, and didn't care what anybody thought about us. When I say that we did everything together, that's exactly what I mean. School, partied, drinking, babysitting, fighting, and more. We depended a lot on one another for a lot of different things, and a lot of different reasons. Still not knowing what God was up to. Secrets shared between us, but only to a certain extent because things that we know now of one another, it's clear that we only told what we wanted to be known. But we had behavioral problems. It would get so stupid at times that we would get kicked out of school. One time he got kicked out of school without me, and he knew he was going to be in some serious trouble when he got home. So he came up with the perfect plan (so he thought) to lay in the middle of the street as if he had been ran over by a car. While lying there a car came up and the person jumped out to see if he was alright. The ambulance was called and his mother also. As they were being transported to the hospital, his mother was looking through his books and found the suspension slip. She must have beaten him so; I know he wished that a car really hit him, after that whooping she put on him (laughing). But I told a tad bit of that story to show how crazy life would get for us at times. Looking back on those times, I know that it was so not worth it. Acting against the rules and having bad attitudes only landed us in summer school, which we would cut up in there too but not as bad because we knew we needed those credits to get back in school, and pass on to the next grade. I really wasn't a fighter and only had two of my OWN and the rest was defending my best friend. I always tried to please people just to have friends. I know you're probably thinking "not Tammy". Yes me. But I would soon learn that I couldn't please or trust everyone. I got lied on, stepped on, turned on, cheated on, but I ignored it and kept on going. LIVING LIFE! Almost every night we would steal my cousin's car and go to the liquor store so we could get drunk. We were definitely a mess, but God was bigger than all the mess that we were putting ourselves through. Thank You Lord! When your life is a mess, that's when people will find a crack to get in and get what they want from you, and will use you up until either you wise up, or they get tired of you and push you away. Much as the devil finds an opening in your life to come in, to try to kill, steal, and destroy. The devil himself knows the purposes that God has set for your life, so with everything in him he will try to come discourage you from it. I am a living testimony to this, because my innocence was stripped from me. And it came through the whispers of NO ONE WILL BELIEVE YOU. Focusing the story back to the molestation that took place with me. I can remember a cousin started having his way with me too. So during this time frame, I was thinking I know for sure this isn't right. Cousins DON'T be that way with each other. Then I think, IS IT WRONG? A cousin's husband took his chance with me one night while I was sleeping. It had become hard for me to get sleep, because I didn't know who would be coming for me once I closed my eyes. As my cousin would be down stairs entertaining her friends, he would be having his way with me. My thought process all warped out of frame. I began to think men wanted Tammy. Not knowing that the devil had set me up. And the devil sure didn't know that God had something for him the whole time . . . all in the same sense tough, I was just a scared, shy, little girl with a GROWN situation and didn't know how to deal with it. So I was darned if I do, and darned if I don't. still, on and on I go as if anything bad wasn't happening to me, I press. He did this until he thought I was at the age to tell, or that I had finally got the courage to tell. I'm really not sure which made him quit, but whatever it was I'm glad he did. One thing I could never understand or figure out is, that why I always had a sense of forgiveness for these people that had harmed me. I couldn't understand how I could be in the company of such people or how it seemed to be alright to be calmed and quite during those times. As I began to think more on the situation, I would often hold myself at fault thinking that I had did something wrong. And readers I tell you that that is the most humiliating feeling, blaming yourself when you've done absolutely nothing wrong. Living with pain and guilt only made things worse. Rerouting a little bit, to show how things wrongful done to you can play a major part of your deciding factors. I was fifteen and dating the neighborhood bad guy. He was very mature for his age, but he was a headache to some, and annoying to others. Either way, him and I shared a long time relationship. And at times when we weren't dating, we would continue to be involved as if we were. We were always a part of what was going on, being in different grades and different schools didn't matter to us, as long as we had each other . . . . at least that's what silly ol' me thought. Being his girl, he would do anything for me and there literally were no boundaries. He gave me gifts, and surprise me with things all the time. He spoiled me and it was surprising, because he was younger than me. As time went on, our relationship would continue to grow. And by the age sixteen, I would be pregnant. Being that age, I was scared but also excited. He surely was happy enough for the both of us about it. Sadly the pregnancy wouldn't last long. Within me being two months pregnant, I started to experience a miscarriage. Not knowing what was going on, I called my best friend with fear in my voice to describe to him, what was going on with me. He told me to calm down and that we were going to figure it out together. By then his mom heard us talking, and he started to tell her of my symptoms and I heard her tell him that it sounded like a miscarriage. In denial and not wanting to believe that, I began to cry. We called the clinic and a nurse gave orders for me to lye back and prop my feet to elevate, to try to stop the bleeding. Then she said, that if the bleeding didn't stop to come into the emergency room. As the day went into the evening and the pain in my belly grew stronger, I finally made the decision to go into the emergency room. On the way, we went by and got my granny so she could be there with me, even though I didn't want her to be because she would be sitting there telling me the truth, about everything and I didn't want to hear it. While lying in the hospital bed waiting on the doctor to come in, still I bleed like a slaughtered hog. "It will be alright" I kept hearing my granny say. I was in so much pain that I remember saying to her "just shut up". Didn't mean harm toward her, but at that moment everything was so painful and overwhelming. When the doctor got in the room and examined me, he assured that it was a miscarriage that I was having. My world stopped for a split second. There was silence, and I couldn't get my mind right. I really wanted my baby, even though I knew in my heart of heart I was too young age wise and mentally to raise a baby. Even still it was heart breaking to know that I wasn't going to have a part of me to love me. Within all that I had to have a slight procedure done to stop the bleeding and get the rest of the baby out. Everyone kept telling me that it wasn't necessarily a baby yet, but I felt that it was and to find out in my later years that it was definitely a baby. A part of me died that day with my child, and being two months pregnant may not seem like a great loss to most people, it was truly a loss that I will never forget. I would wonder for years why such luck feel on me all the time, and why were other women fortunate enough to have their children. Well the little rascal satan had got in again, to make me think I was cursed. And it would be later that I would learn from Gods word that in order for me to bring forth life, I first had to learn to live. I just figured that my boyfriend and I would be good parents to our child. Little did I know that God knew best before the incident ever happened. For a while my boyfriend was mad at me, because he somehow found fault in me of why I lost the baby. As if the stressing behind him didn't play a part in it at all. REALLY? A short while later, he became abusive. He pushed, punched, slammed, on me as if I was a nobody, and he showed no remorse at all. Punching in my mouth until he would draw blood, then walk away like we just had the best day ever. But I allowed him to do these things to me, and let it be fine as long as he didn't leave me. I thought my life was designed to have junk happen to me, to have hurt happen to me, to have people abuse me. So although he was doing hurtful things to be, I would still deal with him because I thought I loved him. My mentality started me to believe that if they don't hurt you in some type of way, then they don't love you. WHAT KIND OF FOOLISH THINKING IS THAT? He went on to get entangled with other women and continued to do his own thing. And that consisted of, whatever ever he thought he was big and bad enough to do. And I would sit back and wait on him time and time again. I kept hanging out with my family and friends to get over the mistreatment of my own life. Thinking that I would start to see someone else, that's what I did. It made me feel better about myself. This relationship was a bit different from what I was use to. And it felt a certain type of way. A feeling that was good, but I was so scared to trust it. This particular guy had been wanting to date me for a while in high school, but I wasn't interested then. Slowly I decided to become his girlfriend. And the longer we dated the closer we became, and as I said before the feeling was scarey but I liked it, and I liked him. We had fun together all the time, he was silly and always made me laugh. At the age of eighteen, I would find myself in the emergency room yet again. But this time I was in full blown labor. Yes you guessed it, I was pregnant. This time around I carried my baby full term and was about to give birth. Through this pregnancy was a lot of crazy situations that occurred during the entire time. By me finding out so early of the relationship that I was pregnant, I thought it could no way be the guy that I was currently dating. So I told him that he wasn't the father and that I understood if he didn't want to see me anymore. To my surprise, he still wanted to date. As time went on and I proceeded to go to the clinic to get prenatal care, it was then that I found out that my boyfriend actually was the father of my unborn child. Needless to say, he didn't believe after coming back to him retracting the first story I told. Strangely we would continue on, and him and my ex would argue, fuss, and fight continuously. By the time I was eight months into pregnancy he told me that he believes that the baby IS his, and that he is going to be there for us to help take care of him. My heart smiled that day because even though we were still together, I wanted him to believe that my child was his and that I made a mistake by misjudging my calculation of term. My boyfriend went through so much nonsense with my ex, that I thought at one point I was going to lose him over it. But he hung in there with me just like he said he would. While in the hospital, after giving birth to our 9lb 13 1/2oz. baby boy, which we named De'Marcus, and nicknamed "Tiga'". And my boyfriend was going to be in the delivery room with me, but he got scared and nervous, so he had to leave out. But good thing I had my mama there too . . . . it was so funny to see him getting weak at the knees, from the mere thought of having to watch me go through that, and see his child come out. Everything was going good. Family and friends was in and out visiting us, bringing gifts and food spoiling us tremendously. One day, while my boyfriend was there with me, a couple of his friends came up to see our baby and they sit around for a while laughing and joking, having a good time. By then they all decided it go see their coach which was in the hospital during that time. My baby's father kissed me and said that he would be back shortly. I think thirty minutes had past, and then he comes back to the room covered in blood. I looked at him and let out a slight scream, then asked what had happened. He proceeded to tell me that the ex-boyfriend was on his way to see the baby, and they got into a fist fight in the hallway, which almost caused them to fall out the seventh floor window. It scared me so bad when he came back in the room because I thought he was seriously hurt. The security guard had to escort my ex off of the premises and told him not to come back. But that didn't stop him, he started calling the phone in hospital room making threatening remarks and everything of that nature. Crazy behavior right? . . . you better believe it. Thinking back on that delivery, I remember it being so painful. I was young and small build, so for such a big package to be pushed out was tiring. The doctor had to use forceps to get his 15inche head out. He was humongous (said with laughter). Couldn't believe it. But I was a big baby myself, weighing in at a whopping 8pds. And then his dad was a nice size, so I guess he really had no choice but to have some size on him. Anyway when it was time to be released from the hospital to go home, his going home outfit was too little so we had to have someone from home to bring something else for him to wear. Shaking my head as I dressed him, I said to him boy you are big and this is pitiful. One thing I can guarantee is that day the nurse laid him on my chest, it was then that I knew what real love felt like. Out of all the loves I thought I had had before, I knew at that moment that I hadn't had love at all. I loved my son so much and never wanted that feeling to end. And his nickname fit his weight, I knew he was going to be something special. His father wanted to name him after him, but I don't like to do that. So I name him close to him without him being a jr. and I gave him my dads middle name, so he could have a little piece of him too. Having my son took away all my worries and made everything that I had ever been through, had been worth it. Taking him home and loving on him daily, became something that I really enjoyed doing. And my boyfriend was the best to us. He treated us so good. I lived with my mom for a little while longer after that, and then I moved out to move in with my boyfriend and his family. To show how dysfunctional we were, knowing that we shouldn't had been shacking up like that. Especially, under one of our parents roof. But it was allowed and we did. Things were good and we were living life, and it wasn't anything that could stop us. We were the perfect couple, setting an example on staying together for our child no matter what. I loved my boyfriend/baby's father, and he was different from all the other guys I had seen my home girls experience with the guys they were dealing with. And I never wanted to feel the effect of not having him take care of our child. Eventually I moved out and got my own place so that we wouldn't have to be with his mother anymore. Being and living on my own, I loved it. It gave me a sense of being grown up and responsible. But before I moved out, I found out that I was yet again pregnant with my second child. So living life for my baby boy, and my child that I was carrying, was a joyful feeling. Plus my boyfriend/baby daddy was about to be deployed off. And I was about to feel for the first time, what it was going to be like without him. We had been inseparable from before he graduated until his deployment. It was going to be lonely for me, and I knew it. Before his departure we would spend all our time together in love land, confessing our feelings and dreams with one another. I would tell him how I couldn't wait for him to get back to the kids and me. Soon after, he would be gone and it was just me and baby boy, and the baby I was carrying. At times I felt lonely without him, then other times I felt I could cope. We would write letters to keep our communication lines open, and he would send me money to help take care of the baby, and things around the house. Finally he would get to come home on a two week break. And during that time, we would plan to marry. Even though a lot of people were against it, we did it anyway. It was December 18th, 1989. We would ride up to the courthouse with our mother's, and I had on the ugliest checkered green and black dress, with a black turtle neck underneath it, and my big belly sticking out. We were a hot looking mess and we thought we were the stuff(laughing out loud). A short time after that, he had to go back to his military duties. He wasn't there for the birth of our second child, so I had her alone. Which my mama was there in the beginning, but she left to go shopping for the baby so while she was gone I had her. A healthy beautiful baby girl, weighed in at 8lbs. and 3 1/2oz. and I named her Casey. I gave her my maiden name for her first name, because I wanted her to still carry the family name even if she gets married. when mama and cousin got back, they seen her laying in the nursery and mama was so happy to see her. We stayed in the hospital for a couple of days. That's when they kept you and made sure that baby and mother were fine to go home. Now a days they deliver and send you on out the door, don't know if everything is legit or not. After getting home and having two children there with me, I felt doubled loved. Having my children I knew regardless of what, I would always have someone to love me. Things were easy going at first, other times would seem overwhelming. My mom would always come through and make sure that we were fine, and that we had what we needed. At night when we would lay down to sleep, baby boy would be in bed with me, all up under me that I barely had room to move. And baby girl would sleep in her bed so peacefully. We were a happy family, waiting for Mr. Dad to return home to us. Motherhood was something totally new to me, and having the two no one ever took time to show me how to be better. I thought I was doing a great job, don't get me wrong. But reflecting back on past times, I realize I could have did some things differently. But I sure did love my babies, it was an unspeakable joy. Mr. Dad finally home with us, I was more than happy about that so he could get the chance to bond with his babies as I have. And he did just that. He loved on them kids with everything in him, I would love to sit back and watch him interact with them. And believe me I say, they loved their daddy. One thing was missing from the recipe of our family. Me knowing how or wanting to be a wife to my husband. I still wanted to run around with my so called friends, and not be a full time mommy. I wanted a break from it all, and didn't know to stay and maintain a home for my family. It didn't last long, because even after the talks that he would try to have with me, it didn't work. I still ran around like a crazy person. He got the nerve built up to leave me, and moved in with his mama. I was sad, but didn't show it and acted as if that's what I wanted to happen. Both of us still not knowing how to fix what was broken; we just continued to be a mess. Through all of that, I started to see my ex-boyfriend again(the one that I had the miscarriage with, the abusive one). It added more fuel to the fire with me and Mr. Dad, and I went on like I didn't care. Readers do you know how miserable of a feeling that is, to love someone so much but you make stupid choices and allow it all to fall apart? It's such a hurting feeling. Mr. Dad and I would argue, fuss, and say things that couldn't be taken back even if we tried. I figured it was over for good for us, because I knew he was getting to the point of giving up and I sit back foolishly and let it happen. But I began to miss him like crazy and I wanted him to be there for our children. Because while we were going through our mishaps, he had strayed away from the kids too. So I started writing him letters, and leaving them in his mailbox. And I would do this on a daily basis, expressing how sorry I was and that I wanted him back, so we could try for another chance to get it right. When he got in from work every day, there would be a letter in there for him to get. But he never responded to any of them, so I started to get worried that it was over for sure. Thinking I was up a losing battle, I stopped writing. He let me know a little while after the letters stopped, that I was one letter away of winning him back. And that he looked forward to getting home from work to find a letter for him, from me. So one letter short huh? As I laugh to myself and shake my head. As I look back on all that craziness we went through, I can truly smile with a happy heart, because it made us the best of friends and great parents for our children. After getting past the divorce and the anger of everything, we would still see each other from time to time. And before he was to be deployed for overseas, I got pregnant. I didn't tell him though, and kept it to myself. I think because of fear because we wasn't together anymore. After he was gone off he wrote to me, checking in on his babies seeing how life was treating us, and it was then that I would let him know in a responding letter that I was pregnant. Of course he denied the fact that he was the father. And the only thing I said to him was, you will see after the baby is born. I didn't argue about it, because I knew in my heart that the baby was his. I kept a gut feeling that my ex wasn't the dad. Getting close to my due date, I went to stay with my mama as I always did when I got close to the end. I needed to be there so she could help me with the other two little ones. Being pregnant this time around was more difficult than the times before. It threw me into early labor. My baby wasn't due until March, but I went in January. Mama couldn't stay at the hospital with me, because she had to go back to work. So by myself AGAIN, I was admitted and put in the delivery room. It seemed as if it was taking forever for anything to happen. Finally the doctor came in and broke my water, but still I would lay there for hours. Dilating, but the baby would not drop into the birth canal. By the time the baby decided to come, all of my fluids had dried and it was torture to try to push anything out. I was screaming and all over the bed, because it hurt so much. The nurses kept trying to calm me and assure me that everything was going to be ok, but I wasn't trying to hear anything from anybody. I had my bottom raised up off the bed, and the nurse came in, looked at me and said, what is the problem? I told her that when I put my bottom down on the bed it hurts me to lay there. She said you can't have a baby with your bottom in the air. I told her as nicely as I could, that we was going to have to figure out a way to do it, because I'm not coming down. When my baby started to come, the doctor had to literally catch her coming out because I still had my bottom in the air, and she was about to fall out on her head. When it was over, the nurses and doctor laughed at me so hard and said in all their years of delivering, they had never had and experience such as that. By here being so premature, doc had told me that she may have to go in the special care unit for the babies. Because he was scared her lungs and other things hadn't been fully developed yet. So that did worry me a little while I was giving birth, but she was a healthy as could be, and she weighed 6pds. And 6oz. with no health problems at all, I got to keep her with me. Again I was filled with joy. I named her Danielle, which is Mr. Dads middle name. she looked like him lying there wrapped in that blanket, and all I could say is that "I TOLD HIM SO". I was thanking God so much that she was fine and had all her functioning body parts. Another bundle of happiness, to take home to meet her brother and sister. And they welcomed her with love and kisses. I would sit back and look at them, and think those are three small human beings, that were all a part of me and they truly loved me. I finally sat at the kitchen table one day, and wrote a letter and inserted a picture of my precious baby, and mailed it out to Saudi addressed to Mr. Dad and waited on a response from him. I also knew he had people scoping out to see if she looked like him or not, or if they thought she could be his or not. But I said earlier in the book, it didn't matter to me what other people thought because I knew she belonged to him. He finally came to his senses and started to claim her. Mr. Dad and I shared a crazy, topsy turvey type of life with one another. It was a bitter/sweet kind of love we had going on. I know a lot of decisions that were made for the kids, were out of hurt of the relationship period. When he was mad at me, he wouldn't come see or get the kids. And when I was mad at him, I would tend to keep the kids from him. We did selfish things such as that, not realizing that we were hurting them more than ourselves. At one point, I didn't want to be a mother anymore. I wanted to give it all up. I felt like the world was on my shoulders, and I couldn't shake it off no matter what I did. And for the choices I was making, I felt it would be better if someone else took the kids and raised them for me. Readers, when you go through things on a mental level it always seems better to give up and run away. But when there are children involved, you can't do that and feel good about it. Thinking to myself, I thought how it would feel if someone else walked in my shoes for a while. Though I had others trying to be like me, and act like me, dress like me, live like me, they didn't know that I was a train wreck headed for destruction. One day I said forget it "I GIVE UP"! making the decision to let the kids go and live with their grandmother for a while. I packed them up and took them to her, dropped them off and went on about my way. Sounds Motherless doesn't it? Trust me, it was the best for them at that time. Responsibilities, no I didn't want them anymore. Running loose and on numbness, it didn't matter what came my way I was ready to take on the world, because I felt as if nothing could hurt me because the very thing that could knock life out of me, had already been done. And that was the death of my Mom. Life's chaotic, but it didn't matter one way or another. I was angry and I know I caused anger in other people that was a part of my life. Before I knew it, a whole year had passed that my kids were away from me. Mr. Dad told me one day that I needed to get myself together and get the kids, because they needed to be with me. I went to get them, but it seemed life was still the same. But in between all that, I started to date someone else. And we would date a while, get married and have a son. My baby boy, I named him KeAlbre'tt Pauley. Big bouncy, bundle of joy, that popped out at 10pds. And 1oz. his father and I would be in a relationship for a while, and he was wonderful to me and the children. But do you think that it was enough for me? No it wasn't. thinking that he could take the pain of my life away, I decided to play the role for a while. And even though I loved him, it wasn't enough for me to want to be tied down into a marriage again. I knew my mother loved him with everything in her before she died. Still I had a demon I had to battle, and no one could do that for me. When I got pregnant with my baby boy, I went into a depressed state of mind. As if I wasn't already somewhat there. But I didn't want any more children and it threw me off guard when it happened. I took three test to make sure that it was positive. Not sure why I thought that God had miraculously healed me from bearing anymore children, though I wasn't taking anything to prevent it either. Yet six years had gone by with my baby girl, and I had all the kids in school. The thought of me starting over was making me terrible sick. It's crazy because after my mom died, I all of a sudden get pregnant. My sister too. So we always felt it was something of her spiritual doing(laughing). I stayed in denial for eight months of my pregnancy, then I had to come to grips that this thing is real, and a baby will be coming soon so I had to pull myself together. Having a good support team system, I was getting through it one day at a time. Then my cousin planned me a surprised baby shower, right under my nose while I was sitting next door with the neighbor playing cards. My cousin was at my apartment decorating for it, needless to say I was in total shock. But we all had a good time with music, laughter, and eating. I was a big whopper being pregnant with him, but it was all baby I really didn't gain any weight. When it came time for me to have him, I went to my regular scheduled appointment and when the nurse examined me, she told me then to get to the hospital because he was so big that he had no more room to grow, and that they needed to get him out. Being admitted into the hospital, I started feeling uncomfortable but I think it was because I wasn't ready for him to come. Because guess what? That would mean more responsibility. I had so many different feelings through the whole pregnancy, that my moods were unpredictable. Something came over me, as I was lying there while the doc's and nurse's figured out exactly how they were going to perform the delivery. And it was a feeling of peace and I felt ok all of a sudden. I think it was my mom, because she was always there for me with my other babies, and with this one she wasn't there physically . . . but she made sure that she was there spiritually. Time went on and baby daddy had to go back to work, but the neighbors were there for me and the kids. They looked out for us all the time. And it helped me a lot to not have that overwhelming feeling that I would always had. So I was beginning to believe that this relationship was going to work out. I trust that we both were holding on to the hope of it working, wether it did or not. But this would be toll taking too on both of us. I just had to realize that I wasn't good for nobody. I needed to be by myself, just leave all relationships alone. I was poison to them. But I slowly learned that, I couldn't give anyone else love because I was looking for the love of one man, in many men. And that was the love of my father. No matter how hard he tried to make things work with us, the final result was splitting up and going our separate ways. Baby boy was 4 months old and I sent him with his daddy, because everything was so messed up in my world. As I write to tell my story, I realize that I made a mess of a lot of things concerning me, and I hurt a lot of people. I truly apologize for whatever I caused to make life living for someone miserable. Please forgive me. We shared our son between the two of us for a long time. And I allowed him to go live with dad for good when he was about eight years old. He had started to follow in the other kids footsteps instead of leading for himself, and it had started causing him to get in trouble. I also allowed my oldest son to go live with their dad, when he was ten. Now let me clarify some things, because I know you that are reading this, probably think I just gave my boys away. It was a mutual agreement between both parties, and it wasn't of any disturbance of the courts or anything of that matter. But it was for the best interest of the children at that time. I never signed my rights over and was/is still a major part of their lives. Because of it, my oldest son is the man that he is today. A God fearing man, and words can't described him. He is a wonderful young man. And my baby boy is growing into an awesome young fella' himself. Even though they were raised in separate households, the five of us share an unbreakable bond. I've shared talks with my boys to find out how they really felt towards me, and they love me and thank me for allowing them to be raised by their father's, so they could teach them how to be men. Which took some stress off my heart, because the devil and people made me feel like I was a terrible mother. My children are my inspiration and my goal is to make them as proud of me, as I am of them. The hurt of my life and trying to deal with it, caused me to self medicate and drink my pain away. Though the same feelings would be there when I woke up the next morning, it still satisfied me at the moment. I would always, ALWAYS party like a rock star, even when there was no partying left in me. I had always surrounded myself with people or alcohol, it helped me to become more numb to face ME everyday. And honestly speaking . . . a lot of days I didn't want to wake, just so I didn't have to take on another day. But something on the inside of me kept me fighting a little while longer, especially at my lowest points. It was a drive that would help me get up and go another round. I never would sit down and think to kill myself, but in all reality that's what I was doing. Killing myself slowly. The feeling of loneliness played a huge role of my being. I began to think that my life was designed to be bad, to be corrupt, and to be unfulfilled. It had gotten so bad, that it started to become scary. Like a whirl wind coming in full force, with me against the odds. But I learned to pray, I knew praying would be the only thing to save me from whatever I was going through, though sometimes didn't seem to be getting any better. For those of you reading, and you think that your life is a mess that can't be worked out, or you think it's just no way for it to be fixed, here are some things that you can do to get your path redirected on a more positive path.

1. CHOOSE: Decide if you want the change to happen.
2. SEEK OUT WICKEDNESS: Which is the very root of what is causes you to feel unworthy of living.
3. STAND ON HIS PROMISES: Receive and believe what God has said about you.
4. P.U.S.H: Pray until something happens . . . and it is then and only then, will things start to change.

Sometimes we have to live life upside down, in order to learn to live right side up. Now I'm going to throw this thing in reverse for a bit. Readers follow me as I take you back. I give thanks to God for allowing me to have my children with the best two men in the world as fathers. Even through my life being as raggedy as a can of sauerkraut, he saw fit to have those two men come into my life and give me wonderful children. As they were awesome men back then, I wasn't capable enough to see that. What matters to me it that, we share a friendship and we can talk to each other on a mature level, and there are no hard feelings from anyone about our past lives together. God is good and he knows just what to do, and when to do it. So to speak any negative words against either of them could not be done then or now. I pray that God always continue to bless them in a mighty way, and that their cups are continually running over with things that are desires of their hearts. So I personally take this time to thank my children fathers. Thank y'all for putting up with me. Sometimes, things that happens in our lives are not meant to be understood. And we spend a lot of time trying to figure it out, when we should just move on from it. I always wanted to have my children by a good man, because everything that I had gone through with my own. My dad wasn't there for me like he should have been. And it caused me to feel a certain type of way about him. I never understood how he could have me as his child, but never saw fit to come and see me and spend time with me. At times we lived right across the street from one another, and he still never made real effort to come over to visit with me and my children. I carried a chip on my shoulder for him ever since I was old enough to realize that he wasn't being active in my upbringing, or being a part of my live period. I would long to hear my dad tell me that he loves me. And he would never say it, unless I told him first. With everything that happened in my life, my dad never knew about it because he never developed that type of bond with me to know anything on a personal level. Still hurts my heart to this day, that he died and we wasn't any further along with one another then, than we were before. I remember loving him so much that I dared anyone to mistreat him, or degrade him in my presence. The sense of feeling that way overwhelmed me, because I didn't understand why I should give such protection of him, when he gave none for me. It's very important for parents to be a vital part of your children lives, because it does determine how a child grows up and live life for a moment, or a lifetime. When children feel abandonment from someone, especially a parent that's when they go looking for love and comfort somewhere else, and it's usually in the wrong places. Where did that strong love that I had for my dad come from? Why did I value him the way that I did? Why did I keep trying and trying? I realize that's just the way it is with our relationship with God. He reaches for us, time and time again even after we have turned our face from him. He continues to pursue us anyhow. God wants us so bad, and we don't comply it breaks his heart, but he doesn't give up on us. That's how I was feeling about my dad. I figured that if I kept on trying, then eventually he would come around and play by the real rules of being who he was suppose to be to me. I never felt that protection of a father from him. And I thought that's what "good" dads did, protect their child/ren. But if he was never taught how was he going to give it to me? The connection between us was so poor, that I didn't call him DAD, DADDY, DA-DA, none of those words. But instead I called him Dwight as everyone else did, or I would call him double D. now at this point, I want to make some things perfectly clear because I don't want anyone to misunderstand me, or misinterpret my words, or think I'm bashing my dad. My book is geared towards telling the truth about my life as far back as I can remember, and tell it exactly the way it happened, so that someone reading this can heal from a broken relationship with their father. Or for someone to understand a little better about why the relationship between them and their dad wasn't as strong as it could have been. Because if you never find the "ROOT", it can't ever be plucked out to get rid of. I can remember as a little girl, my dad brought me a bike. It was a big huffy cream and brown bike. It had humungous tires, and a huge brown seat. When I tell you I was so proud of that bike, no one could tell nothing that day. It didn't matter if someone tried to make me mad, it wasn't going to work because my daddy had just brought me a present. It was a very special moment for me.

I tried to ride that bike until the wheels fell off. I remember that was the first things I known him to do for me. Even when I tried to reach back in my mind to find something that I may have over looked, because I didn't want him to be a dead beat dad, I couldn't find anything. He would give a little money from time to time, but not enough to amount to anything. To even go past the him, the relationship with my granddad and myself, it had a gap in it. I'm speaking of my dad's father. From what I can remember, he was a mean man. He was mean to me. When I would walk down the street to visit with him, he would yell at me, curse at me, and he also was distant in my life. What would bother me the most, is that we ALL lived in the same town, in walking radius of one another. But it was if we lived thousands of miles apart. I just couldn't get over the fact of that to save my life. I would question many times of how could I love the both of them so much, and they showed such little interest in me, as their flesh and blood. Now knowing that God had given me a loving heart. Time kept going and the world kept moving, so I had to move right along with it.

When my granddad would yell at me, it would scare me so bad that I would take out running from his house, all the way back home with my feelings hurt. I didn't understand at that time that he had an illness, which was Alcoholism. But in my mind, I would still think (how could he treat his granddaughter this way)? As time went on, he would die. So I had to attend the funeral, because after all he was my granddaddy. I can recall myself crying, and yelling out "granddaddy, granddaddy". And truthfully I didn't know if I really felt hurt, or if it was the way I thought I had to act because it was a funeral. I figured I loved him because I was a part of him, and that I was suppose to love him. I never really got to know him, to lay out my own feelings concerning him. I was so confused about the whole situation, and never spoke a word to anyone about it because I figured they wouldn't have the answers that I was seeking. I can imagine how you as the readers are thinking right now. Probably asking how could I speak this way about my family, or how could I seem so cold hearted. Truthfully speaking, at that point it didn't matter because my heart had turned a certain type of way for him and my dad anyway. So going in a little deeper, my dad had brothers and sisters too, and I didn't have a relationship with them either. Almost as if I had no connection with that side of the family. I knew their names, but that was about it on that part. My grandmother from that side was a short, dark skinned, bow-legged lady, and my dad looked a lot like her. Anyway, moving right along.

I know that things in life happens for a reason, and sometimes it's to better us, and other times it could be to challenge us. But whatever the case may be, we have to take heed for whatever it is. Understanding how a child got left behind, to fall between the cracks of life, wasn't something that I could grasp my mind around. Reading my book, may have you feeling mixed emotions. And if so, it means that you are feeling the same things that I was feeling while going through those certain situations. Sometimes I can't help but sound harsh or harden because I carried those emotions for a long time, with life's happenings. I would be upset but dared anyone else to disrespect or degrade him in my presence. I defended him being an alcoholic, because I felt at times no matter what HE'S STILL MY DAD. I would try to rationalize his absence, and wonder why whenever we did spend time together, it would be because I would do all the visiting and contacting him to make it happen. I don't think he purposely went out of his way to do anything for me. It's as if I loved him so much . . . but didn't. does that make sense? As a young child when I was a round him for whatever reason, I would NEVER disrespect him. Is it that I was taught not to? No that wasn't the reason at all, I just felt in my heart that me being a part of him I had to hold some type of respect. Even with being out hanging with my friends behind the school late nights, partying, drinking, I still would have compassion for him. I remember a time while being out on the block, one of my friends yelled out "Here comes double D". that was his nickname the streets had given to him. When I heard that he was headed in my direction, I ran and hid behind a tree. I'm not sure if I was running away because he was drunk, and I didn't want to be embarrassed by him, or if it was because I was drunk and didn't want HIM to see ME like that. Either way, it was selfish motivation. So regardless of what the real reason was, it wasn't right.

Someone had spoken out in a disrespectful way to him, so I came out from behind the tree and stepped up for him in the words of "WATCH YO MOUTH, THAT'S MY DADDY"! so again, I came to his rescue. During my teenage years, I stayed doing my own thing. And on top of that, I was a crying drunk . . . meaning I would drink and think of all the bad stuff that had happened to me, and would cry for hours and hours. I just couldn't for the life of me understand, why me of all people had all these problems going on in my life. But I would dress my life and myself up as a pretty picture and keep on moving. Many people would tell me that they wished they had my life, I had a lot of people trying to imitate me far as dressing like me, talking like me, doing the things that I was doing, carrying a certain type of way about themselves, trying to be like me. And I would think to myself, ONLY IF THEY KNEW that this isn't really who I am. But I had to continue to live as if everything was fine, because it really wasn't. it would have took a very STRONG person to walk in my shoes, for in fact those shoes became hard for me to walk in. my shoulders always seemed to be the ones that everybody would dump junk on, and I never had anyone to carry my junk to. LOL, I had to be stronger than most because there was no other way for me to be.

Remembering the first time I found out that my dad was sick with cancer. I went to his home to visit him one sun-shiny day, and a friend of mine and me was out riding enjoying the day and I wanted to go see him. We arrived at his place, I knocked on his door but there was no answer. I didn't even hear the dog that he and his girlfriend had. So I proceeded back to my car, and a older male was in his window and asked me if I was looking for Dwight, and I said yes I am. He went on to say that he had been taken to the hospital and he has cancer. Admitting that the news hit me in the stomach like a ton of bricks, and I immediately got sick, and I couldn't drive. My friend had to drive my car to the hospital, because I wanted to be there for him. I had so many things running through my mind, and then I became angry because I didn't understand why no one had contacted me to give me the news of him being sick. When I arrived at the hospital and made it to his room, he wasn't in there and the worse thoughts came to me, thinking he was dead already. So I ran into the bathroom and cried my eyes out, when his girlfriend walked in and embraced me, to let me know that they had taken him down for testing. But still I cried because I didn't want him to be sick, and even though he hadn't been the best daddy, I didn't want him to die and leave me. And I wasn't thought of as a factor to know what was really going on. This was a critical time and again, I was left out. Into details she would go about his illness, and I couldn't keep my composure. Trying to take it all in I started to think of how still to that day, we hadn't become any closer in our relationship. I was hurt and confused all at the same time. During the time of his hospitalization, I stayed with him one night. I helped him to the restroom when he needed to go, I gave him water when he needed it, and as I was doing those things for him, I would say to myself that I can do this. I thought that I could help him, no matter hoe raggedy our relationship was. No matter that he hasn't been there for me, and no matter that he never said he was sorry for all the hurt he caused me to feel towards him. When the truth was, I JUST COULDN'T DO IT!.

After leaving the hospital the next morning, I told him that I would come back after work. I didn't go back to see him, I called instead. Even in our phone conversation I told him I would come back to the hospital for a little while, but still I didn't go. As bad as I wanted to be there for him in his time of need, I couldn't make myself jump in full fledge. I would question if I was being selfish or not. When the truth of my actions were, I still carried the broken heart of the little girl I once was and felt he abandoned me. It was an emotional battle that I was dealing with, and all in one dimension try to get closer to him on his death bed. It was hard for me to go visit him in that way, because I couldn't stomach that he was going through that. I started to feel a certain type of way again, because I didn't want to be sick, I didn't want him to be dying, I didn't want to lose the man that was my daddy, because we still had some bonding to do. It wasn't fair that he was going to die, and we hadn't lived life together yet. Wrapped and torn in emotions, I didn't know how to deal with it all, so I mostly stayed away. The times that I would go, would be so stressful for me that I wouldn't go back for a while. It was if he was fading away right before my eyes, and what child wants to see their parent losing life every day, every minute? I didn't want to see that, nor accept it. When it had gotten to the point that we had to feed him baby food, I couldn't handle that and I wanted no parts of it, as one of my aunts said that it had to be done, so I have to do it I thought to myself, no I don't and I didn't.

A short time before all of this, my dad had moved in with his nephew because of things that he was going through with his girlfriend. Everyone thought it would be better if he got away from her. Because she was meaning him more harm than good. Even though my dad knew right from wrong, he would let certain ones redirect his path from me. Reader's I know y'all are on a roll with reading, but this is one of the times that I am putting the book in reverse. I'm going to explain some of the reasons of where the lack of respect came in for my dad, and not being able to be there for him. It's from when I decided to visit him way before he was sick. When I knocked on the door and he asked, who is it? I replied, it's me. He asked me to wait a minute before he would let me in. he finally opened the door, and he had company. Several people sitting around. But it wasn't out of the ordinary, because he kept a house full all the time. I started to notice that the longer I stayed, the more antsy he got. He couldn't sit still, but I guess he felt he couldn't dare ask me to leave. Being that we never spent much time together. As my visit started to prolong, he just couldn't take it anymore. And he went between the cushions of his couch and pulled out a crack pipe and started to light it up and smoke it right in front of me. Now I am in total disbelief, my mind was saying no I'm not really seeing this, but I knew it was happening. I jumped up from the couch and screamed at him "HOW COULD YOU DO THIS IN FRONT OF ME"? and he said in an unremorseful voice "it's my house, and I'm your daddy, and you shouldn't have stayed too long". Once again my feelings were all over the place. I wanted to know why he kept taking us there, and why was it so hard for him to be the part that he SUPPOSE to be in my life. I left his apartment, and I can't remember when we saw one another again after that. When he had the nerve to disrespect me like that, it mentally ate at me but in a different way from what I had already been feeling. I don't know how many of you readers has endured the same things as I have endure with my dad, but I want you to know that there is hope and there is healing, if you allow God to heal you. Back to where I left off with my cousin taking care of my dad during his time of need. The day that my dad died, I was at work and I kept telling a co-worker that I was going to visit my dad on lunch break. Usually I wouldn't take a lunch break, but he was on my heart so heavy that day and I knew I needed to get over there and see him. But before my break time even came, I received a call from my oldest son saying that I needed to get over there to my dad, because my aunt had called him and said that he has died. I dropped the phone and started screaming, my co-workers all ran in to see what was going on. I told them that my dad had just passed away and that I had to leave. One of my friends called her mother to come drive me, which was right around the corner. When I arrived at the house, they had already gotten him out and carrying him to the morgue. I get out the car as fast as I could so that I could run over to him. One guy asked me if I wanted to see him, and I said yes. As I'm walking to the back of the vehicle they have him in, I couldn't stop crying. When I looked at him lying there, a part of me died too. I didn't know how to feel or what to think. All a knew is that a man named Dwight Lynn Davis, that was my daddy was now gone. Now there was no way for our relationship to be restored, because he would be with me no longer. Guilt kicked in on my part, I knew better than to let him die, without being there for him whole heartedly and physically. I dealt with that for a long time.

At night I would cry myself crazy, thinking how I could have made it better for us. But I let my pride and my hurt get in the way of it all. So now how do I deal with losing a father I never really had?

Another phase in my life that I would have to eventually deal with head on. I wasn't ready to solve the scattered pieces of that puzzle, so guess what? Yep you're right . . . I put that way in the back of my mental closet as well, along with other issues I had hanging in there. Again life is moving on. Still in reverse of my story, I would like to introduce some of you to the name of my mother. Her name was Pamela Casey Gilmore. I spoke of her a bit in the beginning of my book. Readers go with me now as I take you on a journey in the life of my mother, for as much as I know. As I have explained all of my life to everyone that I talk to about her, she was my heart and soul. She was born to the late James Kearny Casey and to Rosetta Hightower Casey, on November 8th, 1955. I really don't know much about her childhood, but I do know that she was raised up in a loving family with her mama, brothers, aunts, uncles, and a lot of cousins that she loved and they loved her.

My mother gave birth to me October 15th, 1970. At the early age of fourteen years old, she was just a young child herself so my grandma helped out a great deal with me. I can only imagine that my mother wanted to still live her childhood life with all her family and friends. I think my grandma made her be responsible still, but at the same time allowed her to still be a kid. As I write about my mother's childhood, it will be strictly from things I was told until I was old enough to remember on my own. I have a lot of memories of spending time with my grandma, and one great aunt in particular. I spent a lot of time with them, and that's not to say that my mom was a bad mom, I truly believe that other family member's came in so strong because she was so young, and they wanted to help as much as they could. I do remember on some occasions that mama wanted to take me with her, but grandma would say no. I don't believe she said no because she didn't want trust her because she was such a young mother, or if it was because she felt like I would be in better care of her hands. Whatever the reasoning were, I stayed home a lot. I can in my memories of how my mama would wear those bell bottom pants, and her wigs she would put on. Or she would wear a low cut afro. To me she was the prettiest woman in the world. She had the most beautiful smile I had ever seen, and she was always full of life. I don't remember mama being pregnant with my sister, I do recall her coming home from the hospital with her (giggles) going up to the bedroom where we slept, she had this baby cuffed in her arms. Laid her on the bed, and as I go in the room to look at the baby, I noticed that she was very pretty. She laid there with dark chocolate skin toned and a lot of thick straight hair. A few minutes later, I would learn that her name is Tawanna. Now that mama had two children to care for, her responsibilities became more demanding. But by us still being in the household with my grandma, I believe she took up time with baby sister too. It was a four year age difference between myself and my baby sister. I don't remember much of her baby years, it seemed she grew up so fast. As time went on, mama would move us out into our own place to live. She made it so warm and cozy for us, and I loved being there with her. We were blessed with a good man as a step father. He treated us nice, and I can't remember him ever being mean to us. Me and my sister loved us some him . . . smiles. Even being in our own place apart from grandma, the child molester would now start to visit our home that was happy. You know it's a shame how someone that you trust and has been treated like family, comes in to take your innocence and take the right from you to makes decisions on your own. Not once, but more than I can count. It was pure betrayal and I didn't/couldn't understand it. Betrayal has been going on in the world for a very long time. It even goes back to the Biblical days, when Judas betrayed Jesus even when he declared he wouldn't. it's the very reason we must be careful about who we let into our lives and entertain.

He made me sad again, confused again, go into a shell again. You even have to be leary of family, because all is not good seeds. What made them think that they could come in and have their way with me like that? What made them think that they could take me innocence? What made them think that I wouldn't mind if they had their way with me? Who are they to take me for granted? Then get up and walk away as if it was suppose to happen like that. Now my hormones are out of wack. I started to crave what my body didn't want. I started to seek unhealthy attention. The question I had was.... WHERE WERE MY PARENTS? Where was my protection? Where were the one's that was suppose to be protecting me from the big bad wolf? Where was my help? As I cried out silently, I was begging for someone to hear me, hear my cry, to listen to what was happening to me. But no one, not one, ever came. Couldn't they see my face? Didn't anyone see my actions? Did I not smell of sexual scent? Instead I was left alone to cope with it, the best I knew how. The very first night that I ever got touched, was I yelling out "Hey family friend come get me"? did I at the age of three years old display any type of actions to make him think I wanted him sexually? NO, I didn't. the mental battles in the shadows of my mind were lifeless. Nothing with life breathing in it, could live in me because I was no longer clean, I had been exposed to the dirty world of lies, deceptions, lust, and sex. How do you move on from such things as that? My mama would go out and party all the time, and on particular night she went out not knowing that she was leaving us in the hands of the molester that kept his part in our family. Also his girlfriend at the time was with him too. As my sister and me lie sleeping in our mama's bed, I could hear him start an argument with his girlfriend so that she would get mad and leave the house. And she did actually what he laid trap for her to do, SHE LEFT! A few minutes after I heard the door slam, he was up the stairway, in the room and at the bed side. The only thing I could think was to protect my little sister from this monster. But I wanted to protect myself also. When he leaned in to touch me, I suddenly got courage from somewhere and jumped up out of bed yelling NO! NO! NO! all I could think about was running and getting away from him. Making it down to the front door and outside running down the street to where the club was so I could get my mama. I ask the person at the front entrance if my mom was in there. Of course he asked who my mother was. I told him, and he went inside to get her for me. She came out looking puzzled and wondered why I was down there for her. Out of breath and crying, I told her what had happened. Headed back to the house, but when we got there he was already gone and my sister still asleep the way I left her. Hating leaving her in harms way, but I know I had to get help. Never knew if anyone ever confronted him or not, because when that night was over that's exactly what it was, over. Because no one mentioned it again. Not to even ask if I was ok, or how long it had been going on, I mean absolutely nothing. How was I suppose to feel after that? Did I question if she my mama cared or not? Yes I did. But it didn't change anything though. I kept thinking of him standing in the doorway watching us lying there. The light in the hallway was on and I had my eyes closed, but opened enough to see what was going on. I was scared to breathe, it was an awful feeling and at the end of it all, no one cared enough to ask me anything. As I think back on that, I shake my head in shame. Did that make mama a bad mother? I asked myself, what makes a bad mother? What are the tell signs that you look for to diagnose someone as an unfit parent? Then I had no clue of what the answer should have been, but now I know that as being a parent that I would do what's in my power to protect my children. Have I made mistakes in parenting my children? Of course I have, but I also know that nothing would stop me from making sure that they are in good hands. Learning to live life a certain kind of way so that the pain doesn't take control, you learn to handle things differently, and you make the choices not to deal with it. When in reality we should face whatever demons we have because they were put into our lives by someone else head on. Sometimes we feel as if it would be better to brush it off and go on, but that's not how we should conduct ourselves especially when the outcome is going to affect SELF. We as a people should always protect ourselves, because if we always leave ourselves vunerable then anybody can come in and do exactly what they want to do to us. Seeking God and doing what he shows us to do, will help greatly in the long run of life. God does things for us that no man nor woman could ever do for one another, the respect of other humans has been so diluted that it is rarely seen anymore. Today times isn't anything the way it was when I was growing up in my childhood. Grown-ups looked out for each other, and when one child misbehaved another parent had the right to discipline that child. During those times, they never let anyone go hungry, they never let anyone be without, standing in the gap really meant something to them. But nowadays, people will turn their nose up to you, they will look down on you, and will participate in the actions of helping to keep another person down. I have truly learned a lot traveling my life's journey. And I am so thankful and blessed that God made me the person that he did, because I've always been a helper, a giver, a give myself away type of person. And even when wrong has been done to me, I still give someone a chance. I know exactly where I got my golden heart from, my Mother . . . lol. Everything about life is not peaches and cream, and we can't expect for it to be. With that being said, we have to know that no matter what, we have a savior that can help us through any and every thing. A lot times we feel as if we have been through or is going through too much for anyone to handle, and our minds begin to take on a mindset that nothing or no one can help the situation, but we must not give place to our own thinking or to the devils thinking, because that will keep us in our unhappy place while trying to get to a better place. So we have to train and equipped ourselves how to make healthier choices, I am a true witness that self destruction is the worst destruction. Let me take you with me on a journey to a town called Clarksville, Tn. I would live there a while with my second husband. And things were good with us, until I started to hang out and meet new people and once again try to live the single life. My husband was an awesome man to me and my children. He never complained much, and very seldom told me No. it was basically anything I wanted he made sure we had it. Why couldn't I just get it right? Why did I do things to hender my marriage? Why wasn't I strong enough to fight off all that was bad for me? Why when I had such a wonderful man that was there with us every day, went to work to make a living for us, and turned the other cheek when I know some days he wanted to knock me on my back because I kept doing stupid things, making crazy choices, that I couldn't at least make us work for the sake of him and the children. Eventually it took a toll on our relationship, and I didn't want to be a part of it anymore so we separated and I went on my way and he moved back to his hometown, with our baby boy. So the life that I "thought" I wanted, I began to live. Always in the fast life, every day in the spot light. Doing my own thing and still not listening to what anyone had to say. Hanging out and making moves with my home girls and home boys, you may find me anywhere at any time. While one night in a night club, which I had gone to solo that night. I met a guy, we exchanged our names and our phone numbers. A few days after that, we began to carry lengthy conversations on the phone and we would make each other laugh so hard, and we always had something to talk about. It was never a dull moment. Finally we decided to get together and hang out. And from that day of spending time with him, would end up in being some very long bad days of my life. In the beginning, as everything does started out ooh la la good and it kept butterflies in my stomach at the very thought of him. Painting a perfect picture of our lives, and he was the painter. I didn't realize that he was using water paint and the colors weren't bold enough to stand the test of our relationship. He wore a very large mask on his face that I couldn't see, or was it that I didn't want to see it? Doctor Jackel and Mr. Hyde type of personality. As I was in this relationship with him, I would see all the warning signs of what was to come, but I refused to do anything about it. I was always one that thought I couldn't live without a man, and when one didn't work out I had another one ready to replace what I let go. So it wasn't a thing for me to keep it moving and have someone up under me all the time. *behavior from my childhood life and didn't realize it*.

I learned to deal and not try to get it right for my children and myself. As I think back on it, it gives me knots and a sick feeling in my stomach. Because how could I be so stupid to have that in my life? Seriously, for whoever is reading this and if you are going through an unhealthy relationship, I encourage now to get out of it RIGHT NOW! It will only lead to worse conditions, and no matter how much he says that he's sorry, and that he will never do it again . . . . guess what? YES HE WILL! Please don't degrade yourself for a man that's not worthy of you. Because any man that is for you and love you, will not resort to things that will hurt you and cause disturbance in your life. We as women are worth so much more than mistreatment, unbalance, and not being loved. Get rid of that unnecessary baggage and move on to a positive path. This man definitely was not near positive for me, he kept me torn down only to try to build me up to HIS standard of who he wanted me to be. I stayed with him until I found strength from somewhere (God) that positioned me to leave him. As scared as I was, I knew it was the right thing for me to do. He didn't like the fact that I had left him, and especially without him having any knowledge of me preparing to leave him. He was furious and wanted to harm me in any way that he could. He began to make unexpected visits to my apartment. And he wanted to run my place as if we were together still. But every time I shunned him away, he would come back stronger. I began to see his appearance change, he started to look different. In a crazy type of way. I didn't know what was going on with him, and didn't understand why he was acting that way. I started to feel threatened whenever he was around. My space, again had became violated by him. It was if he woke up every day with thoughts to torture me and make living hell for me. How do I stop this is what I would ask myself, with no answers to benefit what I was going through, I just kept ignoring him thinking the problem would go away. WRONG . . . it got worse. He stole the keys to my car and apparently had a copy made, because early one morning around 6:30 a.m. the neighbor came knocked on my door to let me know that my car was sitting in the middle of the road. I knew right away that he was to blame for this, because his behavior had been off the charts by then anyway. Another incident that happened while preparing to go hang out with friends, and not spend time with him. He tried to pull me out of a car so he could fight me, and keep me at home to be miserable. I was begging for my life with the others in the car, to not open the car doors for him because I knew I would be in trouble if he had gotten his hands on me. Even though I had friends that were on my side, I still didn't feel safe with him being in my presence. As his demeanor got more and more out of hand, his physical looks would take on change too. I noticed, but didn't pay attention to it much. But every time he would come his skin color had gotten darker, and it seemed his face was sinking in. he looked to not have life running through his veins. A dull grayish color would become what I saw, whenever I would see him. Scarey to look at during that time. White foam would build up in the corners of his mouth, and during those important moments I didn't realize that he had taken on a demonic form. Never really knew what one looked like until that day. I couldn't believe what I was seeing, right before my eyes. I knew I had to keep him away from me. But despite all that had already went on with us, God always sends warning before destruction. Another day when he decided to come and show up, my children were back in my hometown visiting family, my roommate was gone out visiting, so that left me home alone. A knock came on the door, and me being who I am I yelled out COME IN thinking it was a home girl or someone of that nature. As the door opened and he walked in, I was so scared that I stood in place. I couldn't move, and I wanted to scream but couldn't do that either. He then said that he was sorry for all the things that he had been doing to me. Saying that he would like to be friends if we couldn't be anything else. Scared as I was, I was agreeing to everything that he was saying because I just wanted him out of my apartment. As he begin to leave, he turns around look me in my face and says "i still love you" and he walks out. I ran so fast over to the door to lock it, that I almost fell through. I didn't know how things would be between us after that, seeing him all the time, because he would be next door visiting with his daughter, we would speak with casual conversation and keep it moving. (the devil setting me up for the fall). The weekend was approaching and I was planning another cook out at my place. Good friends, good food, good music, and a lot of laughs and fun. As the day came for everything to fall in place, we were getting organized and then it was party time. I seen him walking up the street and came pass my place. We was heading to his baby mama house. A brief moment he stays in there, then back out again to ask if he could join us. I didn't see a problem with it, we're all having fun so I allowed him to come over(satans trap). As the night was nearing an end, I heard him say that he was going to the club with his home boys. But thinking to myself, I'm like "why is he telling me?" I'm not his woman anymore so details of his life doesn't matter to me. Asking if he could come back later after the club, I politely told him that he could not come back. Not knowing what the next day was going to bring, I head on to bed. Morning is creeping in, and the birds are chirping, the sunlight is shining through, as I continue to lie in bed. I hear a knock on the door. Then the knocks turned into strong beating, My roommate runs in my room and says "it's him". So I tell her to let him in, and at the same time i'm getting out of bed so I can handle him in whatever way I needed to, for beating on my door like that. Asking what he want, he asked me to take him on an errand to get something that he had left in his friend's car. And I did. Never should have let him in my car, and should had ever trusted him (correction) I don't think I trusted him, but I believed that I would be ok with him for a short amount of time. On the ride over to where we were going, there was no fussing or yelling going on between us (WARNING BEFORE DESTRUCTION). Of course his friends were my friends because of the relationship that we shared. The fella's and I always joked around, my ex never had a problem with it. But on this day, he did. Well I tell you that it almost cost me my life. He kept asking questions of if I had any plans of getting back with him? And I was informing him that I wasn't getting back with him in any type of relationship. With him not liking and agreeing with my response, he grabbed the steering wheel. Scared to out of my mind, I gained control of the wheel again. I started to pray and ask God to please let me make it back to my place, being that we wasn't that far away. Driving right along and scared, he looked over at me and said, "If I can't have you, then nobody can have you". Then he pulled the steering wheel again, only this time he actually succeeded in what he was trying to do. The car went over into the medium, and we were hit from the front which spun us around to be hit from the back. At that moment I lost all sense of control over my own life. Screaming out for him to call the ambulance because he had the cell phone in his lap, it seemed he was in shock too. He couldn't move and he had the look on his face, as if he couldn't believe that he had just caused this car wreck to happen. It was a blessing that a policeman was at the store, and saw what had just taken place. He sped over to help until the medics got there on the scene to do what had to be done. During the process of waiting, I told him that I couldn't feel my left leg. And I had heavy breathing, which I thought I was going to die. I continued to pray to God not to let me die. I was so scared, and I had never been that scared in my life. Being pinned inside the car, the medics had to use what they call the jaw's of life to remove me from the vehicle. The ride in the ambulance to the hospital was so painful, because I couldn't let my leg lie flat on the bed. They rushed me to the back once we got there, and were thinking that my hip was broken. X-ray proved that my pelvic bone had been broken severely. Snapped apart. Two days in the hospital and couldn't walk. He had his friends calling the hospital asking me all kinds of questions, trying to see where my mind set was. Trying to see what I was going to say about him, and about what happened. Basically seeing if I was blaming him for the accident. Well heck yea I was blaming him, because it was his fault. We as people take things in life for granted, and I took the fact that I was able to walk has use of my legs for granted. Because until I was without use of one, I didn't care as much. We have to be mindful of what we have, and not focus on what we don't have because in due time what we need to have will come to us anyway. Spending those few days in the hospital made me realize just how gone his mind was. It caused me to wake up and see that, if he would do something that extreme that he did mean more harm to me than none. Knowing it before hand, but not really wanting to believe it caused me to be in the situation I was in. who's to blame? Me of course. Even though I didn't think that I had did anything to him, to make him want to kill me it still happened that way. as I replayed everything about our relationship over and over in my mind, I still couldn't believe that this had just happened to me. You never think that something like that can hit your front door, it's like things like that only happens in the movies, or it happens to other people that you know, but you never imagine that it will happen to you personally. Life had taken a drastic change. And I didn't know if I was coming or going. Being in a wheelchair, and on a walker to get around, really had me thrown off. Not being able to jump up and go when I pleased, or doing what I was used to doing on a daily basis, had me bound down and confused. I had to have my friends help me do everything that use to do on my own. Now I needed anyone that could come give help. It was an uneasy feeling, and I didn't like feeling dependent on anyone. So again I would ask the Lord why me? Why was I the one that had to go through another bad chapter in my life? What was I to learn from this Lord? All these questions I had, and no one to give me answers. I felt alone, I felt abandoned, I felt like an outcast that was doomed for the worst. I did have a good support team and they were there to make sure that I was recovering well, and that I had what I needed. On the days that I was alone, was the hardest because it gave me unused time to think. And when I thought, it caused me to feel sorry for myself and the position I was in. I cried a lot, and sometimes slept a lot too. Depression was falling upon me, and it was coming quick. When I was well enough to walk again, I started to hang back out in the clubs. Even though I was limping and barely making it at times, I still would go hang out. Doping myself with my prescribed pain medications and drinking alcohol with it only numbed me that much more. And by the time I made it home, the only thing I could do was pass out. And would pray that God woke me up the next morning. I lived life this way for a long time. As bad as I was living my life, God still saw fit to hold on to me a little while longer. He kept me, and he was ALWAYS there for me. The question is "was I indirectly trying to kill myself"? maybe, maybe not. At that point who knew? Because I sure didn't. I would hate to think I could actually do that to myself. Things were just beginning to take a spiral turn. Everything was going more downhill. My thought process wasn't on point. slowly trying to climb from the black hole that I was lying in, it started to become harder and harder to grip what I needed to hold on to in order to get me out. Taking matters into my own hands, and not trusting the Lord for too much of anything, I dug deeper and deeper, and was getting muddier and muddier, soon it became a task to try getting clean again. When looking in the mirror, I didn't recognize who was starring back @ me anymore. She looked like me, fixed her hair like me, put on her make-up like me, BUT, was NOT me. I was trapped inside there crying to get out. And the more I cried, the more I felt stuck within. Who could help me? Who could I call on? Who's going to be my comforter today, because I need someone? I have a self pity song that I need to sing, please someone come by so I can share the words with you. Can anyone hear my voice singing such a heart tugging tune? Girl can you understand the words that's coming from my mouth? Before too long, I didn't even understand the words that was coming out of my own mouth. It all started to sound mumbled-jumbled, mush mouth. Nothing was making sense any longer. Drained mentally and physically, but would refuel myself up on pills and alcohol. Smoked weed, until my lungs were about to fall out of my chest. Oh well I didn't care, because whatever was going to happen let it happen. Bring on the doom, it's what I'm use to anyway. I knew I had to do something different if I wanted to survive, but what was the "something different" that I was suppose to do. How did I take the steps to get to that point of wanting different? So guess what? I was still stuck because I didn't know how to move my feet to walk in another direction, to change the path I was on. A path of destruction, failure, death. Dying slowly but wanting to live. It was a battle within itself, and me dying was winning. Where was my strength? Where was my fight? It wasn't in me at some points. All I cared about was numbing myself, so I didn't have to feel anything. If I began to feel, I would take another pill, or I would take another drink, whatever it took for me not to take on feelings. So sad but it was true. Oh but God, he kept watch over me, and wouldn't let satan snatch me. Thank you Lord. I was starting to hit rock bottom, and had no place to run. Even though running was so easy for me, and that's what I always resulted to. My feet suddenly wouldn't move. As if I had cement blocks on them, they were heavy to lift. Burden down, the world felt like it rested itself upon my shoulders. I couldn't do this all alone and I needed the will to live. Readers do anyone know what I'm talking about? Can anyone relate to my story? Or am I the only one that has been through something like this, because everyone else life has been peaches and cream always? No I don't think so. Everyone goes through something, and it may not be exactly what someone else been through, but we all have test, trials, and tribulations. So if you're acting like life is perfect, then you need to step back and look at things concerning your life and be real with yourself. Sometimes we think our lives are ok, WHY? Because we have used most of it to cover up all the bad anyway. How dare anyone find out that I was abused, my boyfriend used to beat the snot out of me, or I sold my body for money to make ends meet, oh no can't nobody find out about this . . . (get over yourself, because it's not really about you). What you went through, was to strengthen you and to gear you up for the next person coming through that needed that same kind of help to get out of their situation. I have encountered so many women that has been through the absolute same things as me. I was able to give insight and words of encouragement to help them along the way. and when I began to tell them about a man name Jesus, it made what I was doing for them even better. We need to learn to move self out of the way in order to get to where we're destined to be. Self is the worst key to bad habits, bad beings, bad everything because we will allow self to run the show only because it seems the right thing to do. Making mistakes is not necessarily always a bad thing. Mistakes are made to be a learning tool. If we never make them, how do we learn to better from them the next time? What's yielded process is when you keep making the same mistakes over and over again. And you haven't learned one thing about it. Life can get so cluttered at times that when things start to run together at one time, it becomes overwhelming and chaotic. Not a good feeling, seems that you are drowning. That's how it was for me. While recovering, the trail starts. And of course he told his boat load of lies, and tried to make the court believe that he was the victim. At first the judge was going to charge him with attempted murder, but then as the days went on he charged him with wanton endangerment and causing an accident. Needless to say that he didn't get charged with what he really should have. And he only had to serve eleven months and a day in jail. I have never heard anything else from him since going through the court dates. I always wanted to see him again, so he could explain to me why he did what he did. Why did he try to take my life. And why would he come around and try to disrupt my surroundings the way he did. But I guess it's for the best that we never had the opportunity to have that talk, because it probably wouldn't have went over so smoothly. But I don't hold any hatred in my heart for him, but I di pray that God has dealt with him about what he did, and that he has apologized to someone for it, because he never told me that he was sorry. Once again God came in and got me through that too. By the time I got all the way healed, I made the decision to move back home to Madisonville. A place where I could feel safe, and feel wanted until I figured out what I wanted to do next. Didn't have a clue to what that was going to be, but I had my thinking cap on (giggle). Being at home soon became boring, and I started to realize the reasons I left in the first place. People talking and trying to run your life, and thinking they know more about you than you knew about yourself. I was getting fed up and didn't want to be there anymore, so I was mapping out my plans to leave. Still smoking and drinking like a crazy woman, thinking I was clearing my mind when I was only cluttering it more. I learned that people will judge you for everything that you do. Especially the wrong. Because when you do things right, they don't too much talk on that because they don't want to see you do good. I've been talked about and is still being talked about. The difference between now and then, is that now I don't worry about what people say. I don't stress over what they say. I know that it causes more harm to me physically if I let people stress me out. So I truly handle what people has to bring in a whole different way. my mentality has grown and I don't have that old way of thinking anymore, so it helps me to get further along. I try not to sweat the small stuff anymore, because it's not worth it. I had to sit back and start analyzing what was good and bad, and what was worth my worry and what wasn't. and when I started to get that in order, things took a turn a little bit for the better. I would talk to my sister a lot when I was going through. And she would give her advice to me, and I would listen but never really acted on it. I finally decided to move to Texas where she was, and thought that would be a good move for me. It took me a minute to go, because I didn't want to leave home and I didn't want to really start over. But I did go and lived there for six years. My time in Texas was crazy also. In the beginning I kind of laid back for a while, I didn't want to mingle and hang out too much. My sisters friends became my friends, but still I didn't give myself all the way. I'm the kind of person that has to speak little words, sit back and figure a person out to see if they can be trusted or not. And as we all know, people will most the time be exactly who you want or need them to be, in order for them to get what they want from you. False faces comes in many forms and many colors, and if you're not careful they will fool you. Being false comes with sweet talks, convincing words, and betrayal. People will try to get in where they fit in, and if they feel like they fit in with you, then that's where they're coming to if you allow it. So how can we determine the difference?

1. True friends will be there NO MATTER WHAT.
2. Fake friends are there only if it's CONVIENT FOR THEM.

3. True friends know the ugly chapters of your stories and still CHOSE TO BE THERE.
4. Fake friends will take what you're going through and SPREAD IT TO THE WORLD.
5. True friends will help you up when YOU HAVE FALLEN.
6. Fake friends will WATCH YOU FALL AND HELP KEEP YOU DOWN.
7. True friends don't ASK FOR ANYTHING IN RETURN.
8. Fake friends will come if it's BENEFITTING THEM.
9. True friends will ENCOURAGE YOU to do better.
10. Fake friends will talk you into STAYING IN THE SITUATION YOU'RE IN.

Those are some of things we need to identify when choosing someone to be in our immediate circle. The amazing thing is that I trust God more with my life. I look to him for direction, and to show me things that are not right, and what's not good for my life. I made a lot of bad choices while living in Texas, chose to hang out with the wrong people. Also put myself in harmful situations. I remember one incident where I was hanging out with a guy that was a gang banger, and we were in a sexual relationship. I would ride around town with him, knowing that the rival gang bangers were out to get him. And that meant, get him in any way that they could. One morning we had rode to the corner store to grab a couple of things, and then he took me back to my apartment to drop me off. Told me that he would be back later. It wasn't even thirty minutes after he had pulled away, that someone called my phone and told me that he had been shot at the same store that we had just left from. He didn't die, but I had to immediately thank God for taking me away from that situation, because it could have been me. Stupidly, that didn't stop me from hanging out with him or going places with him. Continuously putting myself in danger zones, for the attention of a guy. Foolish of me to do that. I had no one to blame but myself if anything would have happened to me, and having my children grow up without a Mother. How selfish of me. God must had glued himself to my hip, because it was surely the favor of him on my life. I'm so glad that I was able to go through those things, but even more elated that I was able to make it out alive. I stayed in that dangerous relationship for a while, before I finally got out of it.

Taking you readers back a tad bit. Redirecting you back to Tennessee. As I speak about all the friends that I had back then, it was two females that I would hang out with a lot. We did everything together. Partied, played cards, shopping around. At one point in time we all lived together. We went through a lot together, and we always had each other's back no matter what. We knew we had that kind of relationship that would never die, and that we would most likely have a connection. only one out of the three of us had a job, and me and the other one would just hang out all day, and go into clothing stores to steal whatever we wanted. Then we would make it back home in time, and act as if we hadn't did anything. And we would unwind and laugh about the high adrenaline day we had. Everyone else in the house would be looking at us crazy, because they had no idea what we were laughing at. And it was our little secret between us, and we didn't share it with nobody. All of us hung out together, but we also separated and did our own thing at times. When you share a bond with someone, you try to hold on to it forever. Especially if the person has a good spirit, and shows that they are worth being in your company. Trying to figure out life can be hard at times. And you understand it more at certain times, than others. As we were hanging out and living life to the fullest, it all seemed like nothing mattered. We were very negligent in our priorities, but we made the best of it anyway. While one day lying in bed in the room that I slept in, my home girl came in talking with me. And we were making plans for that afternoon of what we were going to get into. Things began to take a turn within a few minutes, and before I knew it we were engaged in a sexual moment. During the time this was happening I didn't think much on what was going on, but when it was over I was in shock and didn't know what to think. She got up and walked out the room as if nothing had happened, and I laid there going over and over in my mind if I was gay or not. I thought, "am I bisexual"? but to be bisexual, I would have to be gay right? Anyway I prepared to get myself together for the day, and we never spoke a word about it again, and it never happened again, and we went on with life as usual. We have hung out, shared hotel rooms, since then and it was never a tempting to be with one another in that way again. We're not uncomfortable when we're around one another, and we still have a blast together. We have been friends for over twelve years, and that one particular day didn't make me look at her in a different way. Now was it couriosity that killed the cat? Or was it something that was going to happen anyway? Either way, I knew after that I didn't want, or have a desire to be with a female again. Some things in life you look back on and ask how did you allow yourself to get in certain situations, knowing that's not what you really want. But I thank God that he protected my mind so that I wouldn't want to be gay or bisexual. You get all those crazy roller coaster rides in your life, when you're living carefree. I know that a lot of things would have been different for me, had I only lived a little differently. When I left Tn. And went back home, I was tired. It seemed I had been beaten with the handle of life. And had been shaken by the winds of mother nature. How do you keep going when fear knocks you down? Where do you go when doors are being closed in your face? Who do you call on when no one is listening? And when you absolutely can't take another step, who do you count on to give you that extra push? When you realize in life what it is that you really want, then you will know that the a person that enters into your life has to be honest and true, ALWAYS has to be honest with themselves. Whatever relationship it is, has to be based on those qualities, and hold a special value that comes along with the territory. It is some what set in coding that no one ever crosses those boundaries with you, that they can't be trusted. Though that incident had happen with me and my roommate, I believe she knew a line had been crossed and it shouldn't had been. Because the respect of our relationship was so strong, it could have gone very wrong in that room that day. I carried a type of way about myself that at times people were afraid of me. They say I displayed a certain look on my face, as to say "DON'T MESS WITH ME". Not knowing that I was a harmless as a butterfly. It's the reason I say, you have to be very steadfast about what you say you're not going to allow yourself to do, or simply not use the word "never". I had allowed myself to stay in the comfort chair and didn't want to get out, because it felt so good. Anything that was going to make me feel uneasy, or make me think I couldn't accomplish it, I didn't want anything to do with it. For as far back as I can remember that held me back and kept me stuck right where I was. Crippled and didn't know it . . . crippled without realizing it . . . crippled and didn't want to be fixed . . . crippled with a suffering spirit . . . crippled and stuck. Here's a way that you can get through your crippled stage.

A). ANALYZE YOURSELF(Soul search).

B). RESEARCH SCRIPTURES(that fits what ever is going on in your life).

C). STAND FIRM(On scriptures that God has given you).

D). SPEAK OVER YOUR LIFE(I am healed).

E). BEGIN TO WALK(Allow God to strengthen your ankles).
Insert these things in your life so that change can begin to take place. Because if you don't fight for yourself, who will? So many times we as people fail to see the bigger picture of life, and we try to make things more than what they really are at that moment. Questioning God for every little thing, as if he's not capable of doing what he KNOWS HOW TO DO. Everyone in life has been through some type of trial and tribulations, and it seems as if it just goes on and on. Do you ever stop to think WHY? Well let me give you some insight on that. IT'S BECAUSE WE DON'T WANT TO TAKE THE TIME TO WAIT ON GOD. WE PRAY TO ASK HIM FOR HELP, BUT IN THE PROCESS WE GET TIRED OF WAITNG FOR HIM TO WORK IT OUT. WE AGAIN PUT OUR MESSY HANDS IN THE MIX, ONLY TO MAKE THINGS WORSE. So the more we meddle with what God is working out for us, the bigger the hole we dig for ourselves. And before you know it, we are so deep down that we have no other choice but to wait for God to come help us out. Look around, where are all the so-called friends we have? Where is the family that said, "don't worry I got you"? Where is that boyfriend or girlfriend that promised that their love is forever, and that they would never leave you? Where is everybody? For certain they haven't left you to fight this thing all alone have they? I know in a few minutes someone is going to call and ask "what can I do to help". OH!! hold on, I forgot. That reality is if it's not something to benefit them, then guess what? THEY'RE NOT COMING TO YOUR RESCUE!

Learn to trust God, Point blank period. We have to stop settling for just any thing, and start to believe that we are worth way more than what we accept for ourselves. I remember a sermon that my son preached, and he was talking about all the quotation marks, giving the definition of each on and how God would use them for our lives. He was giving demonstration on how we always want to put a period(.) behind everything that we do, or after whatever is going on. And knowing that a period(.) ends it all. It's done, finished and you can't add anything after that. He went on to say that in the areas that we use periods(.) we should actually be using comma's(,) because the definition of a (,) allows you to add more to the story, add more to your life, add more to whatever you need more added on to. I said that to say. When God keeps handing out comma's(,) to you, stop trying to place a period(.) to end what he wants you to keep adding something on to. Until I heard that message I never realized that it was so true for many of us, most of us. When I think back on the incident with the ex that tried to kill me, I knew God was trying to give me a period(.) then but I kept putting a comma(,) in it's place and it almost destroyed me. Readers we must STOP getting our quotation marks mixed up and learn how to use them correctly, and place them as needed. Who is this man called Jesus that I keep talking about? That I keep referring to? Let me tell you who he is. He is a man of Grace and Mercy, he is a man that restores our strength everyday when we feel like there's no strength left. He is the man that places his hand on our eyelids and whispers (you shall live another day). He is that man that is always there to comfort you, when everyone else has ran off. He is that same man that took the clay and began to sculpture something so magnificent in each one of us. Who is this man you ask? He is my saviour, my friend, my father, and I thank him dearly everyday for that life he gives me, and for the life he saved me from, and for the life he has set up for me to live from this day forward. An awesome God is he. He made us in his own image, so clearly he thought great of us to make us in such a way.

PURPOSELY CREATED

Designed with purpose, purposely designed
He said hold still sweet child of mine.
Purposely created, Created for a purpose
reshaped me a new heart and brought it to surface.
Uniquely unordinary, Unordinary to be unique
God broke the mold after making me.
One of a kind, but yet the same as others
I'm someone's child, been a wife, still remain a mother.
You see the cover of the book, but you fail to open and read
do me a favor, know the story before you judge me.
I am human, human am I
I walk my JOURNEY with my head held high.
I trust in God, and he trust in me
I am BLESSED and highly FAVORED by the most high KING.
I am: PURPOSELY CREATED~CREATED FOR A PURPOSE.

I pray that we all start to believe that about ourselves. and we shouldn't allow anyone to come in and make us feel any different about it. And when God has done above and beyond things for you, you should tell of those great things. Psalms 105:1-8 tells us,

(Give thanks to the Lord, call on his name; make known among the nations what he has done. Sing to him, sing praise to him; tell of all his wonderful acts. Glory in his name; let the hearts of those that seek the Lord, rejoice. Look to the Lord and his strength; seek his face always. Remember the wonders he has done. His miracles, and the judgements he pronounced. O decendants of Abraham his servant, o sons of Jacob, his chosen ones. He is the Lord our God; his judgements are in the earth. He remembers his covenant forever, the word he commanded, for a thousand generations).

We must always acknowledge God, because without him our lives would be a crumbling shame. I always wanted to be the best that I could be, but at times it just wasn't in me. Do you sometimes look in the mirror and ask the face staring back at you "who are you"? I've done that so many times, and the strangest thing is that at times I didn't know who was in that mirror. We can be strangers to ourselves, but expect everyone around us to accept and know who we are. No it doesn't work that way. It's very important that we learn who self is, because if we don't know then we can live for who we really are. We walk blinded without direction. We continue to repeat the same steps, and go in the same route time and time again. Because we are lost and we have no sense of getting somewhere, because we don't know where we are going. Not knowing who you are causes you to have a lot of baggage in your life. You carry that with you everywhere you go. It begins to slow you down, and it causes you to look over your shoulder all the time. Baggage will keep you looking for things that isn't there and that will never be there because it's not meant for you anyway. Baggage somehow keeps a hold on us when we want to be released, shackles us, binds us, takes hold of us, mentally-physically-emotionally. And we don't know how to break those ties that has been knotted into our lives. So ask yourself the question: "WHO AM I"? then ask God to show you, then start to seek you out. But be careful in asking and make sure that you are ready for what he will show you, because going through the process of being unveiled to yourself is not a pretty sight. You will begin to see so many ugly scars of life start to appear. You will see the abuse of beatings that someone gave you. You will see hurtful words that were lashed out at you in an angry rage. You will see the face of the molester that took your innocence and left deep wounds in your mind. When self is being revealed, you will see when a father wasn't there for you. And you cried out to have a relationship with him. You will see how your mother would leave you alone so she could go out and do her thing. But most importantly, you will see how you lived your life beneath your worth and you let everyone come in and take advantage of you because you had a trusting heart, and because you thought you couldn't be without a man or woman, you chose for hurt and pain to complete your right then needs. Know that you are ready when self is being revealed, because self may look pretty right now, but deep down and up underneath, self is a deteriating being falling off the very bone that God put together, but you chose to let circumstances and situations tear you apart. I will say that you should appreciate all that ugliness and take it to build layer by layer something smooth and strong. Make a foundation of truth to self, giving you concrete surface to stand on. Things may seem a little scary as you look within self, but be not afraid because God is with you and he has all that you need. Living in fear will hold you back from your destiny, and that's exactly what the devil wants you to do. Give him (the devil) notice that he can't lease with you anymore, and that he has been evicted from your temple. Let him know that you divorced him without him knowing, and that you moved to a new location and that he is not welcomed. Let the pain, the discomfort, the heartaches, and everything else that he brought to you be set free and delivered by the mighty power of the Lord. Not saying that when you give your life to Jesus, and start to trust him, and stand on his word, that it will not be trials and tribulations. What I am saying is that with him in your life and you batting on his team, you are garuanteed to score more home runs, than you would without him.

NO FEAR

Not the spirit of FEAR
but strong as a Lion.
Not the tail or be beneath
but at the top worth while.
Not the borrower, but to lend to the need
he's pouring out blessings, with no room to receive.
Don't be afraid, it's not how you were made
fear not my child, give me your heart to save.
Don't cry, wipe the tears from your eyes
God is too good, for us to just get by.
Not a spirit of FEAR, so don't be afraid
My Grace and Mercy for you, sustains another day.
NO FEAR, BE NOT AFRAID, NO FEAR!

We must learn to be strong, and be steadfast, be unmovable. Trust him with your whole being. God wants us to be like small children that trust their Mothers. And we do trust them to make the right decisions for us, because we are not capable of doing it ourselves. And our natural instinct is to trust even when we don't know the outcome. Something in us tells us that mama will not make any terrible choices for us, because she loves us and she won't allow anything bad to happen to us. That very trust that you have or had for her, that is what God wants you to apply towards him. But the difference between God and mama is, he WILL NOT disappoint you as she would. She's human and bound to make mistakes along the way, even though her intentions are good still some level of disappointment falls in there somewhere. With God it's the total opposite. He is a man that he shall not lie, and he shall do you no harm. And you can bet your bottom dollar on him to always come through for you. You have to give God something to work with, because if you expect him to do all the work, then you're sadly mistaking. You have to give something in order for him to begin to make something. Stop holding back on him, because he won't hold back on you. Anything that you ask him for he will give accordingly. The Bible says: we have not because we ask not. How do we set ourselves up to receive if we never do anything for him to bless us with what he has for us? We should always reach for the better things of life. And we should do it humbly and not with pride, for he doesn't like anything done with pride or selfishness. Sometimes we don't realize that we hender ourselves by things that we do or say. Our actions can be awful sometimes, and we are such a eye for eye type of people. We are not to wrong, because someone wronged us. And we are not to point fingers at anyone, because we definitely don't like when there is three pointing back on us. Staying in Gods way will lead us to a healthier life, and it will relieve the stress on our shoulders because we have learned to trust him with it. I speak about my past in this book and when I talk to people on a daily basis. I share my stories because I don't like to see anyone go through the things that I went through, because I know that there are better choices that can be made. When you bless someone with knowledge that you have, it causes you to leap forward into your future and your mind, your heart, your feet are able to stand what's coming in the next chapter of your life. With all that I had been through, I never imagined that I would be the person that I am today, and never thought that I would have the courage to tell about it. I had realized that I didn't make it to this place by myself, and that God did have me the whole time, and that when I saw one set of footprints on the ground from sunlight shining, it was then that he carried me. And it wasn't even the things that I did to make him do that for me, but it was simply because he loves me, he loves you enough to do for us what no one else would do. To not give him praise, and to not glorify him for that would be a shame before him. Life is crazy at times, and we don't want to deal with the drama of it. Going through it makes us acknowledge that we need help other than ourselves, because we are the ones that made a mess of it in the first place. So readers I suggest that you come to your senses and start doing things differently, so that you can different results. Because when you keep doing the same things over and over again, you will keep getting the same results. When I give advice to people when they ask for it, and sometimes I give it even if they don't ask. Giggles. I always come from an angle that I've already experienced. What do we look like trying to tell someone about something that we haven't been through ourselves. Telling the experience of someone else, could be false information. So I really try not to take it from someone else story and keep it in my own front yard, because that's what I know. That's some of the wrong in the world today because folk talk a lot about what they don't know. Don't have a clue. It's the reason that we need to feed ourselves with everything that we can get. It's just like listening to someone give me the word of God, giving me words out of the Bible. But if I don't know that for myself, that means I have to believe what is being told to me. Why? Because I haven't studied to show myself approved with the word. That's why it's said to try the SPIRIT by the SPIRIT. And when it's not right, it will definitely let you know. Don't be afraid to pull back from things unnecessary for your life, and don't scared to say no when it needs to be said. Lets learn to stand up for ourselves so we will stop being ran over. It's up to us to pick and choose our battles, because at the end of the day some of the battles we chose was NOT worth getting in the ring to go rounds with. And we feel as if we have to be the champion of everything, to lose in something or to someone would make us look as if we couldn't hold our own. Well I'm here to tell you that, sometimes backing out of the fight, and ringing the bell makes you the heavy weight champion. That comes back to choosing wisely the choices we make, because it does holds some sort of leverage in your future. When we're young we make a lot of bad choices, and we are peer pressured too. And no matter what we have been taught we still go out in the world and do our own thing. Hanging out and doing things that we wouldn't normally do, now you're locked up, in the hospital, or in the grave. For those of you reading this book and you have children that are acting out and cutting up, don't give up on them. Though the task may be hard to go through, but that is one battle worth going through(fighting for your children). If you give up on them, then they won't have anyone to stand in the gap for them. They will feel unwanted and will continue to be disobedient. Same way with God. We act a fool and go astray, he's still there for us. And he never turn his back on us. I know we make him so mad at times, but he keep right on believing in us, and cheering for us to come on across the finish line into the victory of our lives. Why not trust God? Because the people in our lives fail us every day in our faces, with no shame about it. And we continue to be in the midst of them, but we're so afraid to trust God. With a lot of stumbling blocks, and more heartache than I thought I could bear, I knew I had to trust in someone that would not keep failing me. And with the more I kept falling down, the more God made his face available for me to see. Readers I tell you that calling up on the name of Jesus is the best thing that any one of us can do. I love him so much and wouldn't trade him in for nothing in this world. Trust him people and never let anyone tell you that he not trustworthy, because he is. My story of my life is not pretty, and I wasn't always at my best as you have read. But I will tell and try to help someone with their life, so that they don't have to endure the things that I went through.

My time being lived in Texas, I encountered a lot of people and I should have had my radars up to detect what I needed to know. Because there were a lot of so called friends, that try to do me in on purpose. People that got close to me out of wickedness, and with the intent to harm. When I saw what was going on, I would separate myself and go about my way without them. I loved the experience of all that I encountered while living there. Wishing that I could go back and undo some things, (because if I was thinking before doing) my choices would have been way better than what I chose. Again we learn and move on. One female that had befriended me, we would be together every day hanging out. I met a guy that would later become my husband. He was actually dating her sister at the time, and I would talk to her sister from time to time. But we weren't close like me and ol' girl. Sister's daughter would babysit for me sometimes. And he would bring the kids home in the mornings, but we didn't talk to one another. He would send the kids to knock on the door, and wait for me to open and let them in. then he would go on his way, and we never said or did anything out of the way to each other. Unlike, what other people thought about us. I couldn't worry about what others were saying, because I knew the truth and it wasn't anything going on between the two of us. It's the very reason that I don't like for someone to be all in my face, but then talking negative about me when they're not with me. Granted, we all have had our part in talking about someone else but there is also a time to grow up, and leave all childish things behind. People don't want to do that, because it will cause them to take responsibility for their actions. And when folk want to run around wreckless, they chose to stay in child's play and toss the ball around on the playground, and still at the end of the day, DOES NOT take responsibility. What I dislike the most is that when people blame others for their actions, or blame them for not having a good life, or blaming them for not taking their hard earned money and giving it all to them. Those type will try to make you feel bad and drain you all at the same time. And before you know it, you have been bamboozled, looking like (what the heck just happened). Just as in the Bible, when Judas told Jesus that he would NEVER turn against him. And when it came down to the wire of being ask if he knew Jesus, he said no. Judas supped with Jesus, and dranked the finest of drinks with him. And he turned his back in the most important time. And even though Jesus knew that Judas would betray him, he broke bread with him anyway. That's exactly how we are with everyone that comes into our lives. Though we know that they are no good for us, and that they will stabbed us in the back, and through us under the bus. We let them come into our space anyway. And when they start to show who they really are, we still try to give that benefit of doubt but they just keep going and going and we (ourselves) are the ones that end up hurt. We could save ourselves a lot of heart ache if we only trust our first instincts. But, we as human beings and being fleshy, we long for relationships, and friendships. We try to make the best out of the worst situations, and what I've learned in life is that as much as we don't want to lose certain things, and certain people truth is it's best to let it go. Speaking for myself, I wished that I had analyzed my ex-husband more closely. As I said before, we see the signs but choose to get involved anyway. And then when it starts to go sour, we pretend as if we didn't know a person was that way. I believe we just hope for the best, and in some type of itty bitty way we think we can change them. And compromising is out of the question, it's not going to happen from a lot of people. They are just who they are. Readers I know that there a lot of you out there that has experienced the heartbreak of not having friends, or that special person that you love so much STOPPED loving you back. And wether it is past tense for you, or if it's happening with you now, know that you can move on and not regret the choice you made to do so. Never let anyone or anything dictate your life, because as you allow them to stop your dreams, they are pursuing theirs. So if you feel a certain way in your gut, please follow it.

Just as my relationship with Mr. J, it was too many boundaries being crossed and it followed us everywhere we went. The night, that I went back to his place with him, after he showed up at my door step unannounced, while I had company already. I was already schedule for a bus ride back to my hometown to visit with my family and friends, the next day. He would be the one to drive me to the bus station, and wait with me until the bus came. During that time we would say our sad goodbyes, and see you when you get back, and be good while I'm gone. All the normal things that couples say to one another, when one is about to be absent for a while. We had made the decision to be in a relationship, because we figured that we would make a great couple, despite what other people thought about it. After my week vacation, I loaded up to head back to Texas.

With long bus ride and being hot and frustrated, I couldn't wait to get back home so I could see my kids, and relax, and see my sister. And I did just that. Later that night, I would go spend it, and was even more excited about the night to come being able to spend it with him. We really enjoyed one another that night. We actually had talks about making our relationship more permanent, at least those were the things that he would promise me. I chose to trust him until he proved otherwise. I knew he had been with another woman while I was gone, because there was evidence in several rooms of the house. Not ever saying anything until sometime later, which came about after him saying that he was being faithful to me. I expressed to him that I saw things that told a different story about what he was trying to make me believe. And I kept seeing him, I didn't break it off because it was something about this guy that I really liked. I can't really put a finger on what it was, but I was digging him. One thing I could never figure out, is why he couldn't let one woman satisfy him, but he had to have several on his team. Not realizing that we were SOUL TIED…which means that whatever that something was that grew us to one another, is what had us bound with bondage with one another. I learned about soul ties years later through a woman that hired me on a job at her place of business. And when she begin to explain some things to me, it was then that I started to understand the behavior that I had for this guy. And was so ready to get rid of what was connecting me to him. It was such a drawing to him that at times it became sickening and I knew that it wasn't right nor normal. I would pray and ask God to take those desires away because I was doing myself a lot of harm mentally, while he went on about his way not caring if he hurt me or not. Guess that was that player blood in him…but I COULD understand that part, me being that way myself when I was ready to play. Life for me was always exploring and trying to adventure on new things. When I got with Mr. J I had made up my mind that, I was going to settle down and just be with him, because I was getting tired of the wild life. And thinking he was ready too, only to find out that he wasn't. Being with him made my heart ache all the time, he would always do something to cause that pain to me. And every time I asked questions, he would have explanations that sounded so convincing that I would believe him. He was a sweet talker, he had that way of saying exactly what I needed to hear to know everything was going to be ok. I was so wrapped up in this man that I found myself doing things that I wouldn't normally be doing. While we were supposed to be together, he moved in with another woman that he worked with. Claiming that they were just friends and she needed a roommate to help with the bills. So our communication lines weren't as strong as it had been. One night when getting off work, from the Hospital I had to get another ride because he didn't show to pick me up. My mind was racing and I couldn't take it no more. I gathered my click of women together and walked around to where he was living, oh yea I forgot to mention: the one he moved in with lived right around the corner from me, literally. She was on the main strip, and her house had to be passed to get to mine. Talking about being BOLD he did that. I grabbed me a knife from my kitchen, and we proceeded on our mission. Getting to the house I could see that all the lights were out and it was only reflections from the television. My first instinct was to knock on the door and ask for him, you know get him caught up. But the more I thought about it, I knew that he would lie his way out of it like he did everything else. So instead, I flatten two of his tires on his car. I almost did hers too, but why? She could only make a decision to be with him from information that he gave her about himself. Readers, that's why it's very important of knowing who to let into your life.

Even though we can't really tell from the first couple of times of meeting, but we as women have this feeling that we get deep in our gut, and it's called a Womans Intuition. And it usually leads us right in what we were thinking in the beginning. Along with the Holy spirit, it's a source that we need to listen to very carefully. It will save a lot of heartache in the long run. Truthfully speaking we are taught to trust people, until they give us reason not to. We must learn to PRAY-STUDY-WATCH. Pray to seek understanding about the person, study his/her actions of any red flag signs, watch to see what habits they have, or if anything carry consistency with themselves in ways that can be trusted. It is the small signs that we have failed to stop noticing. We've become such a product of trusting that it has blinded us, even from the one's that has hurt us time and time again, we allow them to gain that comfort zone with us, only for them to strike and hurt us again. So for the other woman to accept the things that Mr. J was telling her, and for her to open the door for him to enter her home, she had trust for him. So I couldn't blame her. So after I slashed his tires, we all began to run. Getting around the corner we stopped, bent over in laughter as we tried to catch our breath from running away. It was funny to us that I had actually done that and didn't have any remorse about it. I honestly wanted to do more than that, but I didn't. After we made it back to the neighborhood, we sat in the yard chilling and drinking beer and still laughing about the situation. The word angry would not begin to describe the feeling that I had for him at that time. I wanted to see him face to face so that I could slap him a couple of times, and scream so loud in his face until his eardrums busted. I wanted to do things to make him hurt the way that he was hurting me. But somehow I knew at the end of it all, it wouldn't have made an ounce of difference. Considering the fact that I had just had a long day at work and then a hilarious night,

I figured it would be a good idea that I carry myself on to the bed because I was absolutely exhausted. Early the next morning I awoke to get my day started, with cleaning and had vaccumed while the kids slept. Around 9:30 a.m. I look out the living room window and see him sitting in his car out front of my place. Scared to come in I guess, he sat there for a while. Never did I go out to invite him in. I did once or twice go out on the balcony to let him know that I see him out there. Still mad at the fact of what he had done the night before, it was best that I didn't approach him right then. After doing my chores, I came out onto my balcony to catch a breeze of fresh air and he was still sitting out there. I know he wanted me to talk to him, but I kept silent with a thousand thoughts running through my mind. At one point I ask him "why are you here?" with no response from him, right then I didn't say another word to him.

LOVING YOU

Love is a roller coaster ride that leaves your stomach in knots
An eternal feeling, that never stops.
Love is like air from a mountain breeze in the morning hours,
The days of spring, the fragrance of flowers.
Love is the results of two hearts compelling as one, with trust,
friendship, loyalty, and fun.
Love is what I want us to remain, rekindling and never stopping
the burning flame.
Loving you and you loving me, then why can't we be at peace and
free?
Love is real that I know, I've been there before, and still want to go.
Love is the hurt that we sometimes go through, I'm suffering now
because I'm so in LOVE with you.

Tammy L. Casey-Hickson

Finally I heard him say to me that he wanted to talk. Thinking
we really didn't have anything to talk about, I kept sitting there.

Because the way I felt about it, is that he made his choice of what he wanted. So I kept refusing to talk with him. Because I knew that I allowed him to do so, I would believe his lies and forgive him. And that is exactly what happened. I began to be involved with him again. Dumb? Yes I know, but I did it. As a result of no trust being in the relationship anymore, I questioned everything he did or anything he said. I was starting to regret the fact that I let the relationship go with the guy I was seeing before him. For the reasons of, I knew that that guy really liked me and he did things to show it, and I never had to question his actions concerning me or anything else. I knew by the way that Mr. J's actions were making me act, that I had made a bad choice to be with him. But again, the energy that we shared was so strong that I couldn't leave him alone. Readers you must understand that I was hurting on the inside, trying to deal with this man. The heart will have you playing tug of war with life and sometimes you're not going to win the tugging. With all the signs, and with all that we had gone through, and with all the heartaches, and all the questions, and with all the gut feelings I had, I ignored it all and married him. You ask why? Then I didn't understand it, but now I can tell you that we were connected by sex ties. Two people that shares chemistry between one another, is connected by the first thing that tied them together. And with him and I, it was sex! It was explosive sex, and it was sex that couldn't be waited to have the next time. We shared sex on numerous occasions during the day, and it kept us entangled in this web of deceit. It became for the both of us, that it didn't matter what would happen as long as we had one another in our live. A sad situation, but it is true. Our wedding ceremony was wonderful, it was a beautiful day. Our family and friends were there to support us and I was happy it was going to be a new start, a new chapter for us. As much as I tried to change him and make him a better man, it just wasn't happening and it was making things worse between us. Still trying to hold on and keep my family together, I would hang in there. Thinking with my energy of connection and not letting my mind do the searching, I found myself getting deeper and deeper in debt with my feelings. The most unbelievable words that he said to me one day, is that he do what he does "cheating" because I don't expect anything better of him. I expect him to be out splurging himself to other women, so it's the reason he does. Yea, exactly what I thought. It's amazing how we allow ourselves to be taken through abuse, no matter what type it is we give room for it to happen to us. It's in some format of a way that we lose ourselves, but yet still holding on to the mere thought of hope being around the corner. God sets before us wisdom, and knowledge. He gives us tools to maneuver through the maze of obstructions, but with our already know it all attitudes, we close the lid and lock the latch on the very help that was sent to set us free. Sometimes we as women look for pieces that we think are missing, when in reality God never intended for us to have what we are looking for. While we WASTE so much of our lives searching for this and that, if we'd only stop to realize IT'S NOT SUPPOSE TO BE, we could detour ourselves to save a lot of pain. Remembering to stay focus on what's really important, and not get side tracked is the most helpful tool of all. And admitting to ourselves that sometimes along the way, yes we do need help whether it's from God, Family, Friends, or neighbor, we need it at times. And YOU have to be real to YOU!

~PIECES OF THE PUZZLE~ (UN-PUZZLED)

One piece, two piece, three piece, four, can't find the fifth piece, it's here no more.
Is it really gone? Or am I too blind to see? That the piece that's missing, is in front of me?
Just when you think you got what you need at hand, in the blink of an eye it's through your fingers like sand.
So don't look for the fifth piece because it's not there.
Your life is not a puzzle it's a blueprint with heirs.
It may seem like a jigsaw when life's pieces don't fit
But God made it that way, so he could make "YOU" not fit.
So one piece, two piece, three piece, four, STOP looking for the fifth piece, because it was never yours.

Tammy L. Casey-Hickson

Being married to Mr. J was challenging. We had our good times and we had our bad. The bad would always seem to outweigh the good. There are times that I can reflect back on, and say "ahhhh yes, those were the good ol' days. People always like to think that you are bashing, or putting another on blast when you tell of things that happened in life while sharing it with that particular person. No, that isn't true at all. The fact of the matter is that a story has to be told in order for a healing to take place. Especially when you've been hurt in such a manner that only written words can tell your life's journey. My tales of my ex-husband and I, are to help someone else in their struggles, and to let them know there is a better outcome of what you think may be a hopeless cause. And truthfully speaking, we all live our lives in different ways, with different thinking. And even though we go through our struggles differently, we can still give that needed help of encouragement, and

Let it be known that God is the key to all things, and with him ALL things are possible. It is definitely hope and a future for your life, and it is worth living no matter what you are going through, no matter how dim the light may be, there is HOPE. I believe the hardest part of my marriage to him, is when I discovered that he may have fathered a child with another woman. Going through our problems as usual, fussing and endless arguments, he would be the one to leave the house every time because he's tired of bickering, REALLY? I guess I was doing it as a workout regiment to lose weight. (Laughs). As he run away as usual, during one of our episodes I stretch out in bed to watch television. As I am lying there trying to take my mind away from such a bad day, the intuition kicked in. something kept telling me to check his jacket pocket. It was a jacket that he wore to work every day. I ignored it, and kept watching my show. But the feeling was growing inside me more and more. Finally I got up, I sat on the side of the bed, and I remembered the saying "if you go looking, you will find". I knew that my suspicions would not prove me wrong. Going into the pocket, I had no idea what I was in store for. Never did I imagine, nor was I or could have ever been ready, for what I found. Inside the jacket there was a small opening, and in that would be a white envelope from the Child Support Unit. Readers let me tell you that I signed for this packet, when the mailman delivered it to our door. You will read shortly why it is a wow factor moment. After signing for the mail, I never thought anything out of the norm because he would receive letters from that division, on occasions. I laid the mail on his night stand and proceeded on about my business. Never assuming, that it contained very important information. As I began to take the papers out of the envelope, my thought process was thinking I was about to read something pertaining to his previous children. But it was then that my world would come crashing down, into pieces that no man could possibly count. With a blown mind, I stumbled backwards and had my hand in a feel my way to the bed motion. Sitting there stunned, speechless, the tears hadn't started to flow yet and I believe it's because I was in shock. I had to read the letter a second time to make sure that it actually had my husband's name, as the guy in questioning. And there it was again, yes it was him, his name hadn't disappeared from the paper as I wanted it to. He was being summoned to go in to have a blood test done, because he had been named as the father of a child. And then….here came the tears. I felt as if I had been hit in my chest by a ball and chain, and all my breath was knocked out of me. Of all the things that he did to me, I would still believe that he wouldn't father a child while being married to me. Again the anger start to build inside me, I wanted to go on a rampage to shred him a part. He wasn't there, he had gone to run the streets, and the thought of that brought more tears. I had nobody, my sister had moved back to Kentucky. All the ladies I went to Beauty School with, wouldn't understand because they were having relationship problems of their own. What was I to do? At that point I knew that I wasn't going to be able to sustain any activities with my children that evening. Mentally I wasn't able and I didn't want to take any frustrations of his wrong doings, out on my children. I set a plan in motion to bathe them early, feed them, and put them in bed. I had a small talk with them to let them know that mama didn't feel good, and that they had to do all these things earlier than usual because I needed some me time, to get my thoughts together. So I needed them not to disturb me. My oldest daughter has always been a concerned person, especially when it comes to me. She asked in a trembling voice "are you ok?" I said to her, I will be. With the kids taken care of, I then made phone calls to him and he didn't answer. I tried numerous of times, still no answers. With the last call, I left a voicemail to let him know that I knew about his situation. He still didn't call me back or come home right then. But I knew that it was a message that he thought he would never hear, and with that I know it made him even more timid to come home. When I couldn't get any answers from him, I then dialed to reach out to the girl that is accusing my husband of being the father to her child. Oh I'm sorry, I forgot to ask...did y'all get where the wow factor came in at? Ok for the ones that didn't get it. Remember when I mentioned about the envelope that I had signed for? The packet that got released into MY hands? That was the same packet that contained the information about him being named as the child's father. I couldn't believe that all this was happening. With ringing in my ear, as I wait for someone to pick up on the other end, someone did. And I ask to speak with the young lady, but the voice on the other end told me she wasn't there. Advised me that she was her mother and was there anything she could do to help. I explained to her who I was, and the reason I was calling, and it was all a shock for her too. She knew of my husband because her daughter had told her about him, but they never knew of a wife. He had told the young girl that he was single, and that he didn't have a woman at all. I never had a chance to speak with the young girl because she wasn't living in the home with her mom any longer. After ending my tear jerking conversation with her, I went down to the corner liquor store to buy me something to drink. I felt like that was the only thing that would take my pain away. Though I was praying to God at the same time, I think the liquor was more so to numb me. I got back to the house and turned the radio on and started to listen to slow jams, pondering in my mind how could he have did this to me. The shock didn't come from him cheating and having an affair, but it was the fact that he was having sexual relationships with protection. That said to me that he didn't care enough about me to protect his self to not bring back diseases. I thank God that didn't happen. As I was drowning my sorrows in the bottle, I heard him put his key in the lock and I never changed my composure. He walked in slowly as if he wasn't for sure what he was about to walk into. House was dark, and soft music playing, probably had him thrown off even more. He sat at the end of the couch were I was lying down, and he tried to put my feet in his lap. I kicked at him and told him not to touch me. The talking and explaining didn't start soon enough for me, so I ask him WHY? That's all I want to know is why? With tears rolling down his face, he began to tell me the story. Which ended up not being the real story, of course not why would he start being truthful now? In the midst of it all, the yelling and screaming, the crying and the drinking, I found myself in an unusual position. Though this bad thing was happening to me, I was consoling him. I was so confused in my mind that I didn't understand it myself. I found myself wanting to make love to him more than before, because I thought that would satisfy his urges to have sex with other women. Crazy me, yes I did that. Regardless how hard I tried, it wasn't helping and our marriage was dying day after day. One day I woke out of my sleep and ask if he would take the children and me to the bus station the following week? I said to him, rather you do or not I will catch a cab, but the fact is I'm leaving you. So every day I would set into motion my plans to leave, and I was moving back to Kentucky Because it was home and I knew I would be safe. There I would have my family and friends to help me through this. I began the packing process and every day he would walk through and just give me a look that I can't describe. It was if he wanted me to go, but then he didn't want me to. It didn't matter because I knew I had to go. My sanity was at stake and I couldn't bare it anymore. So away my kids and I went back home. About three weeks later we made contact with one another. I can't lie, I did miss him like crazy. Because he was my husband and I wanted everything to work out. Another reason I think I tried so hard at it is because my other marriages had failed and ended in divorce, and I didn't want that to happen again. I was living with my granny, going to work every day and trying to get my own place. The kids were happy back in school with their old friends and family, so everything was going smoothly. But then I decided to let husband come give my hometown a try. I figured he wouldn't come to my turf and show out. For surely that is against all the rules, right? Things were good, it's like we were headed for a new beginning. He landed a job and now we're both working trying to get back on our feet. Didn't see any signs of him sleeping with anyone, we were always together. But something that I learned is that…if someone wants to do something bad enough, they will find a way to make sure it happens. Eventually we moved into our place and I decorated to make it feel like a home. The kids were excited to have their own bedrooms again and be able to enjoy the luxury of a place to call ours. All the while I'm thinking we are bonding for a better future, and thinking he was all into me again, like he used to be when we first met. But it was all a fantasy that I had made up in my head. A little while later, months down the line we received a phone call from the mother of the child that he had conceived, while back in Texas. She wanted to know if we could take the child and keep her for a while, four years to be exact. She was making plans to go back to school to further her education. The thought of taking that child made me sick to my stomach, because how could I raise a child that he made by cheating on me. So my initial answer was no, and then I thought I would pray about it. Through my prayers and trying to be civil about a situation that happened against me, I figured that if we didn't take her no telling where she would end up living. With the history of how they were living, it wasn't a good one. No matter how bad the situation was, I had to remember that the child was innocent in it all. We planned a weekend trip to drive to Texas to go get her. This would be my first time ever meeting her or the baby, and I think it would be his second time seeing the baby. By the time she contacted us to ask for our help, the child was already two years old. I knew it would be hard for her to part with her and I thought it would be hard for the child to. But the strangest actions I seen from both is that it was easy for them to let go. It was if she was happy and ready to get on with her life without the child, I was so confused by this. But she was young and I believe she was afraid of being a mother right then at such a young age. While there we had a chance to visit with my sister and stay at her place, and we were able to see our church family we had while living there. When the day came for us to leave, I thought to myself that I was taking on a responsibility that I didn't know if I was ready for it or not. Returning back home, there we would start the next day with a new member added to our family. Quickly my kids fell in love with her, as she did in return. It was taking me a while to swallow it all and take it in. I knew I had to buckle down and do what I needed to do, because she was there and Texas was a long drive to take her back. Eventually I started to loosen up, because she was a sweet child, and she was lovable, and any and everybody that was affiliated with us loved her. How could I go wrong taking on this challenge? Maybe he'll see that I really want our family to work and stay together. It didn't stop him from doing what he had been doing. Me taken care of his daughter and providing her a place to live. feeding her when she was hungry, buying for her with my money when I didn't have to. Consoling her in the middle of the nights when she would have bad dreams. Enrolling her in school, and taking her and picking her up from school. Being the one communicating with the teachers about her progress and other things. And even keeping her in my home, after we split up AGAIN and lived in separate apartments. That wasn't enough, let alone still taking care of my own kids doing all the same things for them. He still went out and continued to cheat and be with other women as he pleased. I have fought other women and argued over this man, and it was all so pointless. While working in a neighborhood store, I had to interact with the public. And I saw a hundred different faces a day. One day I was working and a familiar face came in. didn't think much of it, and she paid for her stuff and left out. Less than thirty minutes later, she was back in the store with another face that I had seen before. Only this time neither one of them was buying anything. And I noticed that they were letting all other customers pass them by. I asked, "Can I help you" so she stepped up to the counter. She asked me how long had my husband and I been divorced? I told her that we weren't divorced, and what is this all about? Folding her arms and scared to really say what she wanted to say, finally she said that he told her that we wasn't together and that we had gotten a divorce. They had been seeing one another for a while and that she was pregnant with his child. When I tell you that my stomach was in knots, but I couldn't let her see that in me. I tried to keep my composure as best I could. Thinking to myself, he has did this again knowing everything we've been through. I came together with a plan between her and I to set him up in the crossfire that he had started. He had to pick me up from work, and I wanted her to be there to confront him in front of me, with everything that she had told me earlier. And she did that and of course he denied it all. He said he didn't know the motive of why she would chose him to say all those things about, because he hadn't been seeing her. She gave me so much information about personal things, that I know he was spending time with her. He would ride her in my car, let her smoke in my car and I didn't allow ANYONE to smoke in my car. He was meeting her at motels and her friend's houses just to be with her. While lying to me, giving me other names and places of where he would be during the times he was out. I thought I was at my wits end and couldn't understand why he kept doing what he was doing. What was really his problem…geesh! Splitting up again, it felt like we were playing a childish game that wasn't a promising end for me. I tried to go ahead with my life, but we continued to play cat and mouse with each other. A year later the baby girl's mama came back to get her, and took her back to Texas. And Mr. J and I remained separated. Time came for the other child to be born, that was said to be his. We never knew exactly what date he was born, but it was January sometime. Without hearing anything from anyone, I was sitting at home and my friend called. She blantly said, "You need to apologize to your husband because he is not the father of that baby that is being put on him. I said that wasn't the point of it. The principal of the whole thing is that he slept with her and he allowed himself to be a candidate. Going through the process of all that, really took a toll on me. It drained me literally. I didn't want to endure anymore heartaches. So I prayed for myself to get the courage to release him and let him go. To keep him out of my life for good. Finally getting the courage to go file for divorce, allow the lawyers to process the papers to send to him while he was living with another woman. He tried to deny the fact that the papers had been sent to him. It took him almost two weeks to sign and send back, he held up the process of the divorce taking place and I didn't understand why that would be hard for him to do because he was running around like a wild forest animal mating with all the female genders that would let him. But finally everything took place and I was free of that marriage. And looking back in time on things today, I can honestly say that, that was the best five hundred and seventy five dollars I had ever spent in my life. I would not change anything concerning that relationship because I know that I had to go through muddy waters and the mind blowing and heartaches to have leverage to stand on, to not allow myself to endure such pain again in my life. Granted we all are going to have things happen to us, because it's all a part of life, the truth of the matter is that we don't have to settle for what we once went through ever again. When we allow ourselves to be opened up and taken by God, and begin to stand on his word and know that it is true, we then can begin to search out ourselves and ask God to transform us into what he want us to be. Knowing that we don't have to be in unhealthy relationships, wether it be (boyfriend/girlfriend-husband and wife-siblings-parent/ child-friends-family) no matter what the connection is between you and someone else, NEVER-EVER fall prey to being tied to that situation in such a way that it will hold you in bondage to the point that you feel you can't break free. Don't allow what has happened to you, determine who you are, who you were, and who you're going to be. God always had a designed purpose for our lives and it's not what everyone else wants it to be. My life started out untampered until someone made the choice to shatter me, and bruise me, but never imagined that they would not break me!

The End.

"WALK LIKE YOU HAVE SOMEWHERE TO GO"

Have you checked out your footwork?
How about your notion? Get with it, pick it up
Don't be slow motion.
(walk like you have somewhere to go).
Examine where you are now
Focus on where you're trying to go.
If you don't move your feet, you'll be stuck for sho'.
(walk like you have somewhere to go).
The mind is equipped to guide us in life
Brainstorm, make plans, shuffle your feet right.
(walk like you have somewhere to go).
Old things pass away-we pick up new
Let God guide you, and help you through.
Sometimes our knees get weak, we fall off path
But God is here to help us last.
So straighten your back, broaden your shoulders
You're life was designed by the BEHOLDER.
He wants you to hold your head up high
And have a made up mind, step in your shoes
And start walking like you have somewhere to go this time.
"WALK LIKE YOU HAVE SOMEWHERE TO GO".

"TIME WILL TELL"

Can you imagine all you go through
Considering the fact, it may all fall soon.
Being a black woman in the world we live in
Can't exceed past poverty, is that a sin?
Contemplating on what to do next
Putting your life in perspective, with everything in check.
Sometimes we're blinded by reality, can't see past the light
Your mind is confused and tangled
Tell me, is that right?
Take what you do and do it well
Because if you don't, and let go TIME WILL TELL!
My life has been tampered from a long time ago
Not old enough to say YES or NO.
At times we go through things, and don't understand why
Trying to block out the hurt only makes you cry.
Take what you see and see it well
Because if you don't, and let go TIME WILL TELL!
Intelligence of the mind is a POWERFUL thing
More you know, the more you gain
Always stay one step ahead of the rest

Put on foot forward, and try your best.

Only you can control your life, in this world that goes round

It's up to you to not let anything or one, hold you down.

Be who you want to be

Say what you want to say

Go where you want to go

Stay where you want to stay

But whatever you do, do it well

Because if you don't, and let go

TIME WILL TELL!

"REMINICING OF YOU"

Dear Mama, it's been sixteen years since you've been gone
Even though it doesn't seem that long.
Time has went quickly, but in my heart it goes slow
Thinking back to that day, I wish you didn't have to go.
Every single day I think and constantly reminded of you
Sometimes in this cold and lonely world
I don't know what to do.
You gave me so much LOVE, and so much HOPE
Please send a signal of how to COPE.
You believed in me, as a Mother should
You had faith when no one else would.
For God so loved the world
That he gave his only begotten son, but then he made you.
A Daughter, A Mother, A Wife, thy most precious one.
You were fun loving, cheerful, and had a HUGE HEART
You were STYLISH, and witty, but PRETTY tops my chart.
Hope you're proud of ya girl, with how I'm going about life
As a STRONG black woman, you taught me that RIGHT?
Make the wrong decisions sometimes
But that's no one's fault but mine.

Keep smiling down on us, and sending your touch
Same back to you, HUGS, KISSES, a bunch.
Dear Mama, I LOVE YOU.

"IF ONLY"

If only I had someone to feel like I feel
If only I had someone to know that feelings are REAL.
If only I had a strong SOLID heart
That's never been broken or TORN apart.
If only I had someone to see deep in my SOUL
And understand me, if only I had someone to LOVE me
For me, and not take my KINDNESS for WEAKNESS
And walk all over me.
If only I had someone to UNDERSTAND what life is about
It would be better for me, no SCREAMS, no SHOUTS!